Contemporary Oral Literature Fieldwork

A Researcher's Guide

Contemporary Oral Literature Fieldwork

A Researcher's Guide

Peter Wasamba

University of Nairobi Press

First published 2015 by
University of Nairobi Press (UONP)
Jomo Kenyatta Memorial Library
University of Nairobi
P.O. Box 30197 – 00100 Nairobi
E-mail: nup@uonbi.ac.ke
www.uonbi.ac.ke/press

University of Nairobi Library CIP Data

Wasamba, Peter
Contemporary oral literature fieldwork: a researcher's guide/by P. Wasamba. – Nairobi: University of Nairobi Press, 2015

GR 350
.K4M3

320pp.
1. Folk literature – Study and teaching -- Kenya
2. Folk literature – Africa   3. Folklore – Kenya

I. Title

ISBN 10: 9966-792-53-8

ISBN 13: 978-9966-792-53-2

Printed by

Dedication

I've been debating on how best to immortalize the knowledge, friendships, warmth, generosity and intellectual engagements I experienced as I worked closely with my students, oral artists, fellow researchers, and community leaders in the course of my intellectual growth. I came to the conclusion that the best way to reciprocate this immense support is by documenting my fieldwork experiences in a form that cannot be altered or falsified. I therefore dedicate this book to my oral literature fieldwork family members enumerated above. Without them, I couldn't have come this far. I still count on them to move the scholarship in African oral genres further.

Contents

List of Pictures

List of Maps

List of Figures

List of Tables

Foreword

Contemporary Oral Literature Fieldwork: A Researcher's Guide by Peter Wasamba is based on his rich research experience that goes back to the days when he was a student in the 1990s to present-day, as a professor of oral literature at the University of Nairobi. This experience has taken him to sites inside and outside Kenya. The book portrays patient, painstaking scholarly research. In this connection, it is rich in interrogating and evaluating several works by experts on oral literature—as well as embracing oral expert comments from scholars. In view of the above, the work demonstrates respect for scholarship.

The author's voice is clear, as he seeks to correct false steps on oral literature scholarship. Wasamba points out past colonial researchers for their racist presumption towards African oral genres and contemporary elitist researchers for their haughty attitude towards the subjects of their research. Indeed, he criticizes Western attitudes for the dearth of African indigenous knowledge in education in Africa, as he makes a case for oral literature. Censuring limitations inherent in this posturing, he discusses as he recommends appropriate theoretical perspectives underpinning fieldwork.

As he does this, he discusses oral literature scholarship in Kenya, makes a case for the study of oral literature, as he casts broadsides at the colonialist who sought to kill it. In the process, he censures some pioneering Kenyan scholars who even posited "that a lot of material had been collected and what was needed was analysis and not further fieldwork. Methodologically, they were suggesting that data collection, and analysis, are different research activities that can be handled separately by different people in different locations and epochs" (14). He however pays accolades to Henry Anyumba, a pioneer scholar and inarguably one of the finest scholars in oral literature in Kenya, for his "tremendous contribution in laying the foundation for systematic oral literature fieldwork in Kenya, and possibly in the East African region" (15).

The book is written against the backdrop of Africa's confusion with regard to the place of oral literature in the face of the rest of the world, where oral literature exists in conjunction with new literary forms. Wasamba argues that the oral and the written literatures are complementary literary forms. Throughout the work, the author underscores the universal dimension of oral literature as he demonstrates its particular attributes. This is important, for there are voices once loud but now somewhat muted suggesting that this art is peculiar to Africa, a kind of special contribution to "world literature." Further, he argues that it is traditional and dynamic, indeed resilient and adaptable, as it fulfils significant functions at all times: "entertain and educate, uphold morals and preserve traditional knowledge and cultural identity" (10).

The book is useful to scholars young and senior, local and foreign-based interested in conducting fieldwork in Africa, as it suggests tips on rapport creation, clothes and footwear suitable for research, taking into consideration terrain and weather as well as culture and religion in the research area. Further, it discusses human boundaries in the field as well, reminding the reader of research tasks such as "transcription and translation" through which the research ensures "data hygiene and post-data analysis"—that is, "meaningful data analysis" founded on "full transcription". The book of course is not about important tips, but about meaty and weighty issues such as discussing seemingly antagonistic qualitative and quantitative approaches to oral literature research and recommending that the two approaches be blended.

Demonstrating how central fieldwork is to the study of oral literature, Wasamba devotes a chapter to a discussion—peppered with his oral literature research experiences in the field such as working in areas of raging armed conflict—on fieldwork ethics, challenges and strategies. Practical fieldwork experience is the bedrock of the book. He analyses field research, delving into ethical issues that once in a while place a researcher on the horns of dilemma. He uses snippets garnered from his experience, such as the ethical dilemma in which he had to choose between research confidentiality and civic responsibility.

In the process, the book discusses the place of theory, arguing for a positive attitude towards theory, as it discusses a number of theories from which a researcher can choose the appropriate one or the ones to use in the field. Yet, as he does this, he emphasizes the centrality of methodology in fieldwork, making this categorical statement garnered from his experience:

I have met good researchers who are more comfortable working
from their offices in the universities rather than venture into the
field. Such scholars cannot guide young researchers in fieldwork
even if they are professors because fieldwork only respects
grounding in methodology and not academic titles. (41)

Consequently, he devotes a chapter to a discussion on
methodology whose components include interviews and
observations. In the process, he implies that some false steps on
oral literature scholarship can be corrected through "clear
research methodology, detailed background of the texts or
incisive analysis". His rich research experience informs this work
that deals with pertinent theoretical and practical issues relating
to oral literature such as its relationship with several disciplines
making it "multidisciplinary." Throughout the book, he argues
and emphasizes that oral literature is multidisciplinary or
"transdisciplinary," cutting across a number of disciplines.
Indeed, repeating and underlining that oral literature is
multidisciplinary explains the recommendation embedded in the
work of a need for collaborative research into this "borderline
discipline" (21). In this connection, he graphically shows in a
series of circles on the one hand oral literature intersecting with
on the other hand: anthropology, folklore, history, linguistics,
medicine, philosophy, and religious studies (22).

For oral literature fieldwork to be successful, he implies that
researchers should be mature, experienced and participatory as
he challenges researchers to "build bridges of understanding" and
"complete the circle of understanding between oral artists,
communities, and fieldworkers to restore trust, promote

ownership and reduce the cost of research" (35). In the process, he discusses "participatory fieldwork" as "a way of identifying with and understanding the community under the study" as he cautions fieldworkers against "outright activism on behalf of the host communities because it may make their findings doubtful due to partisanship" (36). In this context, he points out how students benefit from fieldwork through involving them in the process of research, exposing them to diverse cultures and encouraging them to understand the self. He complements this discussion with personal experiences in the field—persuading us that students and teachers will find this discussion and the experiential dimension beneficial as they prepare to undertake or as they engage in fieldwork.

On the whole, this book should be of great help to such researchers, as it reflects the author's philosophy on the need for continuous oral literature research to keep pace with the dynamic nature of the genre. This book is a major contribution to the discourse on African oral Literature in the 21st Century. Researchers and scholars of orality will find it an indispensible guide as they study old and emergent oral genres in a technologically driven society.

Prof. D H. Muchugu Kiiru
Department of Literature
University of Nairobi

Acknowledgements

Many colleagues, research collaborators, community research assistants, students and organizations have inspired me in writing this book. I would like to thank most sincerely the late Owuor Anyumba for introducing me to the joy of living and thinking fieldwork. I would also like to thank Prof. Okoth Okombo for his support and encouragement, Dr. Jennifer Muchiri for proofreading the manuscript, Prof. D. H M Kiiru for accepting to do a Forward to this book, Dr. Getie Gelaye and Prof. Mechthild Reh (Hamburg University, Germany) for hosting me twice at the Institute of Asia-African Studies to work on this book and Prof. Jeong Park of Hankuk University of Foreign Studies, South Korea for encouragement.

I'm also profoundly indebted to my life-long research assistants; Mama Kauchi Chivumba and Mzee Omar Mazuri (Kwale County) and Janerose Sichei, Stephen Kirong and Janeline Cherotich (Mt. Elgon), for adopting me as their 'son' since 1998. I cannot leave out my students. I treasure the fond memories in our many fieldwork trips. The ideas they generated in their reports, and the suggestions they made on how best to make oral literature fieldwork exciting have finally been recognized in this book. I remain grateful to the Department of Literature, University of Nairobi, which gave me an opportunity to develop my career as a fieldworker, and DAAD for supporting my research visit to Hamburg University, Germany in 2007 and 2012. Last but not least, I thank my family, Dolphin my wife, Timothy my son and Joy my daughter for their support, patience and understanding.

Peter Wasamba
University of Nairobi, 2015

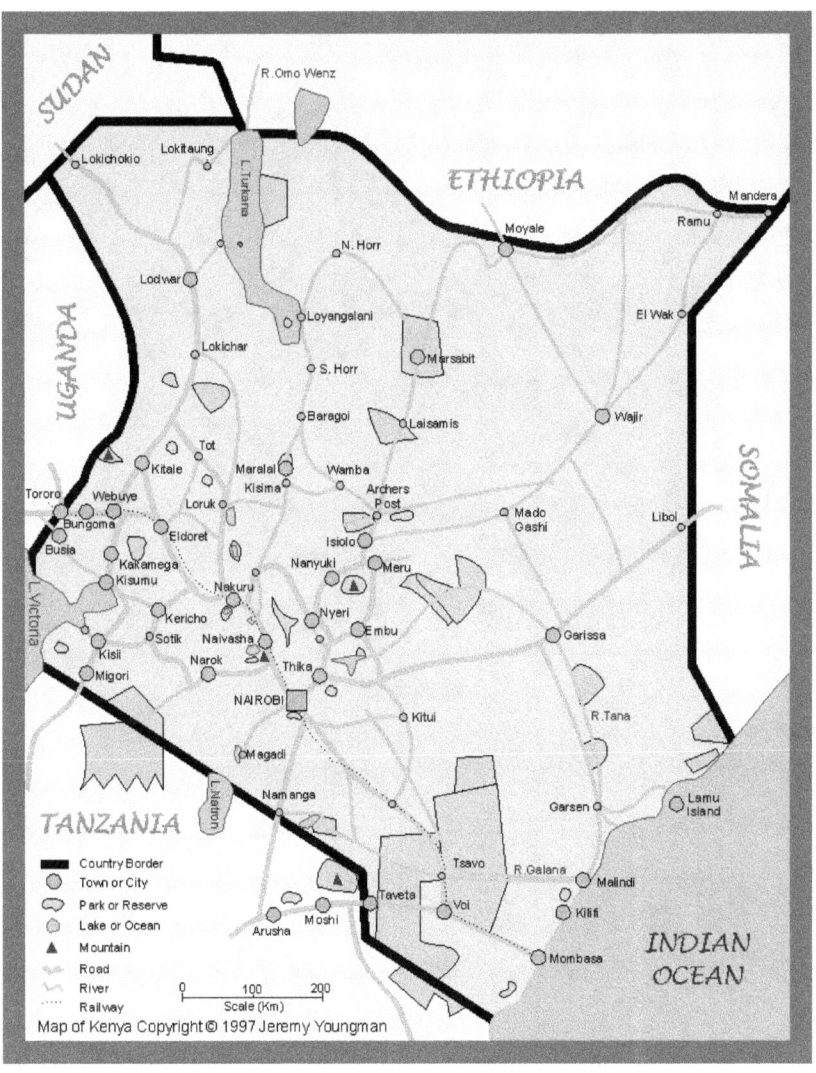

Map of Kenya showing research locations/genres

Introduction

When I was a graduate student majoring in Literature at the University of Nairobi in the 1990s, I grappled with the conceptual understanding of Literature. I was keen to know what I was majoring in. I thought that Literature could be defined. I settled on the definition of Literature as 'all creative works of women and men expressed in words whether in written or spoken form.' I was following the footsteps of Okot p'Bitek and Owuor Anyumba, the doyens of folklore I admired most. With this definition, I was satisfied that I knew and understood the discipline I had chosen. It was spoken or written, creative and produced by and for women and men, young and old. I never imagined for once that Literature would one day include newspaper cuttings, everyday conversations, prayers, gossip, eulogies and other multiple forms that emerge continuously.

My position regarding the definition of Literature has since changed. I now know that the discipline is too multitudinous and changes too rapidly to be ring-fenced by a static definition. As

Gordon ably puts it, a literary work is many things at the same time; it is a reflection of its social climate, a record of the mental history of its author, and a document that can provide unique insights into human experiences and values (166).

In this regard, to attempt a definition of literature would be ambitious in the extreme. There is need to view any definition with some circumspection, given the changing socio-economic and political environment pertaining to Africa. Definitions should allow for constant re-visiting, and scholars should guard against seeing them as inflexible and prescriptive (Kaschula 1999, 56).

If one considers literature to be a credible reflection of a continually changing society, then the term 'definition' may in itself turn out to be anachronism, erring on the side of caution and certainty, rather than seeing literature as an amorphous mass reflecting a fast-changing world which seems to defy fixity and definition as it moves towards globalisation (Kaschula 2001, xii). Regardless of the definition we assign to the hydra headed dragon we call literature, one thing stands out: the art is aural. It is performance that gives form to our ambiguous and complex feelings. Further, it mirrors our thoughts, achievements, disappointments and hopes with deep empathy. Whereas we may use many words like Gordon to explain what literature is and what it does, what ultimately defines literature is its form and place in society. This art has continued to appeal to women and men of all races, generations, and religious persuasions because it mirrors with elegance, intensity and compassion, our everyday experience of life. As a product of imagination, literature is protean and keeps on expanding to accommodate humanity's quest for perfection through aesthetic beauty, philosophical ideals, and artistic truths.

Literature was meant to be and has always remained aural even in the written media. Though appropriated by the literate later on to refer exclusively to the written genre, the term, 'literature,' remains primarily an art of the ear. Oral literature is unique because compared to written literature it exploits spontaneous composition, memorization, adaptation, originality and improvisation, dynamism, involvement of audience and the actual delivery through performance. Literature, since time immemorial, is usually composed to be recited or sung. It explains why poetry is the oldest genre of literature. Although we cannot state exactly when the first poem was performed, it is widely known that poetry has been predominant since early times in Africa, where it was spoken or chanted in various occasions to achieve certain goals. It was a part of religious rites in African communities and is still a vehicle for handing down the stories of a people's struggles and triumphs. The poetic tradition has survived in Africa despite Western-style modernisation. Smith, A. Deavere, in her play *Fires in the Mirror*, asserts that spoken art is the "literature" since "speaking teaches us what our natural literature is" and because everyone, in a given period of time, will say something that is like poetry" (5). Invoking Della Pollock, Laurie Lathem celebrates the power of orality thus: "a story is not a story until it is told; it is not told until it is heard; once it is heard, it changes... a story is not a story until it changes" (81). Since literature is primarily oral, the connection between literature and writing is accidental, and therefore belongs to a secondary phase in the history of Literature (Finnegan 1992, 9). Even in the 20th and 21st Centuries when writing is a major mode of enunciating creative thinking, artists and writers continued to be acutely aware of the acoustic dimension of their writing.

Orality and Literacy

The 21st Century indicates a powerful return to orality, not the primordial orality, but aurality riding on the wings of tradition and technology. Orality exploits the benefits of folklore and modernity to return literature to its original home in performance through Computer Mediated Communication (CMC). Artists in Africa are rapidly reclaiming the oral mode of their living art, sharing their works with the audience while at the same time benefiting materially from their creative sweat. The argument advanced here is not meant, in any way, to downplay the role of writing technology in fostering, preserving and disseminating spoken, acted art. We only affirm that writing was never intended to replace oral performances. It was only introduced to complement and augment the oral modes of communication. Unfortunately, in Africa, the message was miscommunicated through the Western form of education system and religion to mean that only written matter was respectable, official and binding. The spoken art was relegated to the periphery of serious art since it could not be examined in schools and colleges. The way in which literacy was introduced, received and popularised by the dominating powers made it look like written and spoken forms were at war and could not co-exist.

In Europe, Asia, and America, communities retained their traditional forms alongside the new inventions. This has made it easier for them to return to orality as opposed to Africa that still wallows in cultural, linguistic, economic, and political confusion. Nothing in Africa seems to have an African grounding because there is often the temptation to conceptualise ideas in English or French languages with their eurocentric biases and then proceed to graft an African situation to them. As has been lamented before, Africans like the Israelites in captivity by the rivers of Babylon cannot sing the chants of the ancestors convincingly in foreign tongues, hence the unending debate on language, culture, ideology and identity in the post-colony (*Holy Bible*: Psalms, 137).

The debate on language and identity in Africa is tangential to the survival of African oral heritage. While some scholars have lamented the imminent death of oral heritage due to technological advancement, the discipline has gradually reinvented itself and metamorphosed to meet the needs of modern society in novel ways. Indeed, other critics like Malcolm Bradbury talk of the post-modernist movement heralding "The Death of the Book"; which implies a complete return to primary orality (774). This is evidenced in the growing interest in the intangible heritage by the mass media and the emergence of new genres in various cultures. Reality has dawned on scholars that writing, like the digital technology, is not a threat to the growth of literature; in fact it complements the growth of the genre in many ways. Oral literature therefore thrives best in an environment in which orality and literacy operate in partnership and not competition.

Oral literature remains a major genre of literature, especially in Africa where large sections of the population share sentimental attachment to traditional cultures. The term 'oral literature' is widely used, sometimes overlapping with 'oral tradition', but usually with somewhat different coverage and connotations (Finnegan 1992, 9). It is a performed, orally transmitted, and dynamic art form that through the use of language transfers cultural information and values from one generation to another. This definition is not static. It is bound to change from time to time as the genre navigates its existence in a rapidly globalising world that is acutely sensitive to identity issues in communities. Scholarship in oral literature in many universities and institutions worldwide has been going on under different titles and disciplines ranging from 'verbal art', "folklore" to 'oral history.'

History, Religious Studies, Anthropology, Sociology, Ethnology, Linguistics, Rhetoric and Literature, partially deal with verbal art. In this respect, oral literature is like a boarder-operator. It moves between humanities, social sciences and even natural sciences with incredible flexibility. As Alessandro Portelli so aptly says, "oral literature is permeable and borderless, a 'composite genre' which requires that we think flexibly, across and between disciplinary boundaries, in order to make the most of this rich and complex source" (23). In recent times, even medical experts have accepted the age-old knowledge that patients exposed to soothing verses and melodic cadences often develop a positive attitude to life, respond to therapy, and therefore heal faster. Spoken and acted art have the capacity to ease anxiety in patients, reduce perception of pain by scintillating the beauty of life and the need to hang on to it, even when the certainty of finitude looms large.

Oral Literature as Verbal Art

In social sciences, the term ´verbal art´ is used to designate oral literature. The term was introduced as 'a convenient and appropriate term for folktales, myths, legends, proverbs, riddles, and other "literary forms" (Bascom 1955: 245). It was an attempt by social anthropologists of the Malinowskian school to categorize the creative oral expressions they encountered in the societies they studied. Oral literature and verbal art are synonymous. They fall under the broad category of oral heritage, which refers to "works of art, cultural achievements and folklore that have been passed on from earlier generations" (Hornby, 584). Students of oral literature who do not have a grounding in social sciences often confuse oral literature with folklore which refers to the totality of tradition-based creations of a cultural community, expressed by a group or individuals and recognized as reflecting the expectations of a community. Genres of folklore includes language, literature, music, dance, games, mythology, rituals, witchcraft, customs, handicrafts and architecture. Oral heritage, like folklore, is broader than oral literature: it refers to the works of art and culture transmitted orally from earlier generations such as customs, traditions, verbal arts and performances.

In Kenya, whenever we talk about oral heritage, we use the term liberally to mean a collection of oral history, oral narratives, oral poetry, proverbs, riddles and sayings. In its most basic form, oral literature includes traditionally vocally expressed stories, songs, proverbs and other emerging genres that are handed down or created from generation to generation. Tradition is used in this context, not to refer to antiquity, but the dynamic nature of verbal art. Though specific to a particular culture and historical epoch, the spoken and acted art remains largely universal, and ironically, it is stronger in Europe, America and Asia, where modernization is in top gear. Roland Barthes observed this situation and correctly asserted that oral literature is broadly universal without losing its peculiarities. In "Introduction to the Structural Analysis of Narrative," Barthes (1975) argues that oral literature is present at all times, in all places, in all societies. Since the narrative starts with the very history of humankind, there is not, there has never been anywhere, any people without a narrative. Like life itself, it is there, international, trans-historical and trans-cultural (37). Barthes is treating the narrative in its broadest sense which encompasses "different types of storytelling: spontaneous conversational narrative ("natural narrative"); institutionalized oral narrative in an oral culture context; oral bardic poetry; simulations of orality in written texts by means of narrative strategies such as pseudo-orality or *skaz* (Fludernik, 2)".

Oral Literature and Tradition

Some scholars have argued that since it is traditional in composition and rendition; oral literature is trapped in the antiquarian past and cannot, therefore, accommodate modernity, especially in the Computer Mediated Communication (CMC) era. I have interviewed a number of oral artists in some of my fieldwork activities who have also lamented that oral art faces the threat of extinction. Full of nostalgia, these artists remember that in the past, oral poets were happy because performances gave them opportunity to practice their art, celebrate their culture, entertain, educate the community, and preserve their intangible heritage. They compare the danger of extinction facing oral art to that of global warming which is caused by man's rapacious quest for profit at the expense of the environment.

In a tone akin to the negritude poets of the 1960s and 1970s, these artists look back with nostalgia to a time when the environment was green and beautiful, rains were predictable and adequate, rivers flowed gracefully through villages, food was enough and people were healthy, happy and poetic. Greed, scarcity, apathy, strife, drought, disease, wars, displacement, and death have replaced the rosy picture of the past and reduced art to a luxury for the rich. Dirges, laments, and hollow praise songs meant to flatter politicians for monetary gains have since replaced celebratory poems of initiation, harvests and weddings. Rituals to honour ancestors have been desecrated to flatter the rich and the powerful for monetary gains. These developments mark the transition of the discipline that scholars of orality have to deal with. In no way do these changes portend the stagnation, decline, or death of oral literature as the spoken art. In a salient way, they bring out the resilience of the genre.

The salvage school of ethnological tradition was very active in the 19th and early 20th Centuries. They "tended to regard storytelling as a remnant of a disappearing or authentic culture, hence the many attempts to collect and catalogue tales before they disappeared" (Abrams, 138). The treatment of oral literature as dead or dying genre has persisted in some quarters to the present times. Those who lament the death of oral literature, fail to appreciate the fluid nature of the genre in transition. They assume that the genre is fixed and antiquarian hence in dire need of rescue before stagnation and disappearance. Their arguments suggest that only "the 'old' or 'traditional' items from earlier generations are worth attention, rather than individuals who enact and represent the continuing voices of the present" (Finnegan 1992: 217). Scholars lamenting the death of oral literature in the technological age, are looking for the genre as it was in the distant past, instead of locating oral literature as it is in the contemporary society. Faithful connoisseurs of oral literature who walk with it and monitor how it grapples with changes in society can only notice two key factors: resilience and adaptability.

Whereas it is not deniable that in its many aspects, oral literature remains traditional, it is contestable that being traditional consigns oral literature to death in the modern society. This is mainly because the genre is traditional and dynamic at the same time. What is 'traditional' about oral literature is not its antiquity, but the way the verbal art is acquired and adapted by succeeding generations to meet the needs of their times. Ong in *Orality and Literacy: The Technologizing of the Word* asserts that tradition is both deeply conservative and open-ended which enables it 'to accommodate changes in ways that might put to shame scholars of the print culture, who often ridicule their folklore while lusting for the latest novelty' (42). Taking Ong's reasoning further, I discern that oral texts composed and performed by 'traditional' communities in the contemporary society are old and new at the same time. Ong´s use of the verb "lust" is indicative of the disdain he has for the superficial craving for the exotic art that valorises print over performance.

The adaptive nature of oral literature encourages hybridization between the old and the new. As post-modernists passionately argue, what each generation inherits in terms of oral narratives, songs, proverbs, prayers, gossip and riddles is not what it passes on. Each generation modifies inherited texts based on the pertinent issues of the day, quality of oral artists, nature of audience and technological support available (Wasamba 2007, 115). This incremental development of texts is the core of 'tradition' as opposed to antiquity. For example, an oral artist in a performance context creates some connections, which pass to the first audience, who may add new connections and pass the results on to another audience, and so on and so forth. "This passing on of the text from *artist*/writer to *audience*/reader, who then becomes an *artist*/writer for other *audiences*/readers, is nothing new; it is the literal meaning of the word 'tradition'" (Botler, 202 {*italics for emphasis*}).

Oral literature, contrary to the fears artists and scholars express, cannot die due to technological advancement. This is partly because of its ability to adapt to new environments, its multidisciplinary nature, and its resilience as a genre. Since the beginning of the 20th Century, scholarship in oral literature has advanced from medieval interest in origins of cultures to a more focused emphasis on: content, context, meaning, structure and relevance. The contemporary society moves too quickly and is more complex than it was in the ancient past. To remain vibrant, meaningful and relevant, oral literature cannot remain conservative as it was in Homer's day. Recent studies in oral literature have pushed scholarship from the traditional fixation with pure oral literature to applied oral literature by highlighting conceptual issues at the heart of cultural studies such as "intervention, ideology, and theorization of practice as well as the authority and aesthetics of cultural representation" (Baron and Spitzer, vii-viii). Sustainable development rests on the solid foundation of folk wisdom. Development experts, natural and social scientists, including those in the humanities, can benefit immensely by tapping into the insights of scholars of orality and thespians in providing lasting solutions to challenges of illiteracy, disease, poverty, violence and displacements.

Oral Literature as History

An important genre in oral literature work that has not received adequate attention in the past is oral history. This can partly be explained by the assumption that oral history belongs exclusively to history and not literature. Buoyed by New Historicism, this thinking has changed. Led by Stephen Greenblatt and inspired by Michel Foucault's concepts of Discourse and Power, New Historicists bring down barriers that separate literature and history, literary and non-literary texts. It is incontestable that over time, in different places, among different women, men and children of various races, religious persuasions, and traditional belief systems, people have expressed their version of events and interpretations of life experiences through songs, plays, and personal recollections and memories that have been passed down through generations (Slim and Thompson, 1993). These forms of oral evidence, often subsumed under the term 'oral history', overlap and are used interchangeably, with 'personal testimonies,' 'life stories' and 'oral literature'.

A life history is a chronologically told narrative of an individual's past containing recognizable life stages and events such as childhood, education, marriage, achievements, and setbacks. It is a narrative device used by an individual to make sense of a life or experiences in the past. As a qualitative research method, oral history is currently receiving attention from scholars because of its new perspective on the immediate past as a meaning creation space. It stems from the diagnosis of the inadequacies of the established historical scholarship which alienates ordinary people from historical hub. It moves the centre of history writing from macroscopic agents, such as nation, state and society to microscopic ones, such as localities and individuals. The experiences and memories of men and women previously marginalized as the voiceless are recognized, illuminated, and canonized as important data for writing a new history. With the 'crisis of representation', the emphasis has largely been on textual matters but there are a number of fieldworkers who would prefer to see more attention paid to grass-root level actual fieldwork practice (Fabian, 1).

Oral history has been embraced as a libertarian genre. Its distinguishing feature is the inclusion of the perspectives of non-authoritative voices to reclaim the experiences of marginalized groups (Perks and Thomson, ix). With a few notable exceptions (Bird and Shinyekwa, 2003), oral history is not widely used in the context of development. As Cross and Barker (4) propose, however, oral history can complement other sources of data, contest conventional interpretations and attribute alternative versions of processes of change. Long and Villarreal (5) succinctly point out that knowledge is not a fixed commodity owned by 'experts' and elites; it is always a product of social relationships. Consequently, although life stories are inevitably personal, as bearers of culture, the narrators reflect these social relations and counter or challenge dominant discourses and ideologies in a very personal but equally collective manner. Such narratives, looked at collectively, offer the pulse of the community in terms of: what they remember, what they value, what they detest, and their proposals for a better life. Oral history has the potential to facilitate the change process by moving a community from the level of gnosis (*awareness*) to praxis (*action*).

Functionality of Oral Literature

Apart from its amenability to multi-disciplinary engagement, oral literature in Africa continues to attract interest of researchers and scholars because of its enduring aesthetic appeal and relevance. It reflects community life, the spirit of ancestors, and the process of development in changing societies. The texts come from the hearts, minds, and memories of individual artists and other tradition bearers who are not just in touch with reality in their communities but also the changing dynamics in the modern society. Important traditional information or knowledge is not available in our classrooms and text books because

Western pedagogy applied to Africa did not consider folk knowledge valuable. Such important intangible knowledge is embedded in the memories of oral artists, traditional healers, and community leaders, waiting to be reactivated, performed, recorded, studied, perpetuated and applied to daily life.

African communities value performances of various genres of oral literature because they provide education, socialisation, recreation and identity. Telling stories has always been a way to join people together, a way of humanising that which has been dehumanised, of bearing witness and keeping history alive (Lathem, 83). Storytelling is not only capable of humanizing a world in peril; it is also a source of regenerating vitality in the modern family setup. The more we record, study and learn about oral history, the more we understand ourselves and the less we are likely to be drown into the pool of self-hate or bigotry. Manilerd is therefore spot on when he avers that 'lying at the foundation of accumulated cultural heritage from which all knowledge grows is humankind's ability to draw conclusions from the past and project them into the future' (4). The pedagogical value of oral literature that Manilerd intimately captures is rendered through performance. Madison, D Soyini in "Performance, Personal Narratives and Imagination" observes that performance opens the secrets of literature because it invites embodied comparisons between undercurrents that constitute operations of power in our lived experience. Performance promises engagement with what is otherwise hidden, oblique, or secret (Madison 8). Aesthetic experience, which oral literature performance generates in participants, provides experience of the world. 'It counters the sense of removal of the self from the object of study, which traditional schooling emphasizes. The arts, in other words, have the potential to provide an avenue to understanding through personal experience of an otherwise increasingly abstract world' (White, 41).

Oral Literature has remained vibrant and relevant first in preliterate and currently in literate societies because of its capacity to entertain and educate, uphold morals and preserve traditional knowledge and cultural identity. Yet, there seems to be discomfort among scholars in the discipline. They have questions that beg for answers we have not been able to give clearly, convincingly and in good time. Some of the questions that come to mind are: What is the role of verbal art in a changing society? Is oral literature relevant in a digital world? And if it is, in what ways? What can oral literature do to alleviate challenges of disease, hunger, violence, and hate ravaging humble abodes of humanity? These questions continue to torment scholars of oral literature. At the basic survival level, scholars are concerned about career choices, possibilities of getting employment after graduating from the university, and how specialising in the discipline is likely to affect their social standing. Some of my bold students have often approached me, faces twisted with anxiety, innocently curious to know how studying 'stories' can help them get jobs with better career prospects after graduation. Some of these questions, though genuine, are laced with mercantile tendencies that attach temporary material benefits to almost every undertaking in life, intellectual pursuits included.

I have always persuaded my students to understand that oral literature's appeal to the contemporary generation is proof enough of its resilience and value for humankind. The shift from local languages to lingua franca, especially Kiswahili, Arabic and Hausa in Africa, has extended the audience of the oral artists. Addressing contemporary themes such as poverty, corruption, HIV/AIDS, social decay and humanity's quest for lasting peace, have made performances exciting and relevant to young people. Exploitation of form and content of oral texts in film industry, advertising, written literature, speech, religious functions and mass media has revolutionized oral performances. Oral literature performance has also become a well-paying career providing livelihood to many oral artists. Above all, oral literature supports globalization and interdisciplinary collaboration. All knowledge is related, interlinked and therefore, interdependent. There is no discipline that is superior to others because all strive to push the frontiers of knowledge further while at the same time making life more predictable and comfortable for humanity within a given cultural milieu. For those who doubt the relevance of oral literature, 1 can only challenge them to explain how we can secure the future of our past without exploiting the power of our intangible cultural heritage. Using the analogy of a rear view mirror, I challenge them to attempt to drive confidently on a cultural superhighway without a rear view mirror. If you do, you will find yourself a captive of fellow motorists who change lanes and overtake at will as you crane your neck backwards outside the side window dangerously.

Growth of Oral Literature Scholarship in Kenya

At this juncture, it would be helpful to reflect briefly on the history of oral literature scholarship in Kenya, not because it provides a template of the best, but rather because it is an example of how post-colonial states in Africa have attempted to rescue aural art that was viciously curtailed by the colonising powers. In their book *African Oral Literature for Schools*, Nandwa Jane and Bukenya Austine devote a whole chapter to the development of African Oral Literature. It is apparent from their analysis that the development of oral literature mirrors closely the historical and political developments in Kenya as a nation. The major landmarks are the colonial period, the struggle for independence and attainment of political freedom and the development of oral literature as an academic discipline in the postcolonial dispensation. Similar to other parts of the world where there was domination by imperial powers, oral literature in Africa suffered repression. The occupying regimes never allowed African oral literature to thrive under the pretext that it was witchcraft. The real intention was to kill oral literature since it was a powerful mobilizing tool for the masses agitating for freedom.

Yet, when African scholars started championing the revival of African oral literature after independence, they were not in sync with the cultures of the communities they purported to write about. They too had been alienated through deficient colonial education which inculcated in them an inferiority complex and a craving for everything exotic. They had lived and operated from Europe, some of them since childhood, and therefore, were 'rootless' as far as their African background was concerned' (33). Such scholar-politicians conducted research to prove that Africans had their culture and to protest against colonialism and agitate for political freedom. This explains why such scholars confused nationalism with intellectual enterprise. A good example is Jomo Kenyatta, the founding father of the Kenyan state who studied under Malinowski. Bronislaw Malinowski (1884–1942), the enigmatic Polish-born naturalised-British highly esteemed as the father of social anthropology strode the sociological landscape at the turn of the 20th Century like a colossus and influenced many young minds.

Jomo Kenyatta became a graduate of Malinowsky's functionalist approach to understanding the survival of societies. Kenyatta later published *Facing Mount Kenya* (1938), an anthropological work of the utilitarian school. According to Celarent, "Kenyatta's book is an ethnographic rendition of the stable, peaceful Gikuyu and their disturbance by the British, who are portrayed as rapacious, hypocritical, and occasionally rather funny" (723). The same westernization of the emergent African leadership is seen in Kenyatta's contemporary, Milton Obote, the first head of state of Uganda. According to Ali Mazrui (2003), Obote was taken in by the Western civilization that he even named himself after John Milton: "Uganda had for Head of Government a person who had changed his name because of admiration of the author of the great English poem, *Paradise Lost*. Obote became Milton Obote out of admiration of John Milton" (136).

The period from the 1960s to mid 1970s recorded increasing interest in researching and teaching African oral literature in East African schools and universities due to a change in the English syllabus that introduced African literature as the foundation of learning about other literatures. The renaissance in African oral literature in East Africa, known as 'the great Nairobi literature debate' was initiated on 24 October 1968 through a departmental memo. The scholars: Owuor Anyumba, Ngugi wa Thiongo and Taban lo Liyong rebelled against the colonial English syllabus and demanded the introduction of African literature syllabi in schools and universities. In a paper entitled "On the abolition of the English Department", they argued that the primary duty of literature is to illuminate the spirit animating a people, to show how it meets the challenges and investigates possible areas of development (Ngugi 1986, 89). They emphasized the need for a cultural reinvention and revival of Africa's cultural past to help address some of the emerging challenges in independent Kenya (Odhiambo, T, 2004). The rebellion led to major changes in the literature syllabi not only at the University of Nairobi but also at the University of Dar es Salaam and Makerere with oral literature receiving serious attention in scholarship. This radical change influenced Pio Zirimu in Makerere University, and Grant Kamenju in University of Dar es Salaam.

The literary indigenisation revolution swept through the three East African Universities, but it was more pronounced at the University of Nairobi where the name of the department changed from the Department of English to the Department of Literature. The philosophy that guided the curriculum review was based on the premise "that knowing oneself and one's environment was the correct basis of absorbing the world" (Ngugi 1993, 9). The new curriculum "placed East African literature and orature in the centre of the first year, with other Third World and then European literatures introduced in the following two years. The shift from "English" to "Literature" had nationalistic ramifications: by making regional literature the curricular core, the abolitionists redefined the nation (Sicherman, Carol, 1998: 129). No writer captured the mood of the moment better than Okot p'Bitek through his famous publications *Song of Lawino* (1966), and *Song of Ocol* (1967). The publications were a defiant celebration of the rich African culture that the previous colonial English curriculum had either suppressed or ignored.

The immediate challenge was how to teach and examine African oral literature in schools and universities. The spoken art, it was argued by scholars of English literature, could not be taught and tested as an academic discipline because it had no intellectual perimeters. Local scholars out to disabuse such scholars of this notion urgently embarked on the production of teaching material to facilitate the delivery and examination of African oral literature. This led to hurried collection of oral narratives, proverbs, riddles and songs without any clear research methodology, detailed background of the texts or incisive analysis. Graduate students in the Department of Literature at the University of Nairobi did the collection under the supervision of their lecturers and this effort produced the much-needed teaching material. The texts published focused only on the collection of oral texts themselves with scanty analysis suitable for high school students. In 1980s, teaching of oral literature in high schools and universities had taken root. The texts published include Taban lo Liyong, (1971), Roscoe and Ogutu (1974), Odaga A (1982), Mwangi R (1983) and Wanjiku Kabira and Karega Mutahi (1988). The discipline could be taught, examined and graded just like any other, though with a few hitches.

The False Step

This was the first major false step in terms of teaching and the examination, and criticism of oral literature. African scholars realised that it was urgent to re-introduce oral literature in the education system, but they did not ask – "which education?" They ended up bending African oral literature to meet the requirements of written European literature by focusing more on writing for examination purposes as an alternative to preserving the texts in performances. Instead of inviting resident artists to be employed in Departments of Literature, History, and African studies to deliver texts as was the norm in the community, students were occasionally taken to the field to listen to the performances; not to enjoy and learn from them, but to have the ear for transcription, translation and analysis to earn high grades. In many cases, students were not even exposed to the performance experience in the field for logistical reasons ranging from lack of money to lack of interest by the lecturers in charge.

Carol Sicherman correctly observes that, the colonial educational pyramid erected by a brutally rigorous examination system remained standing at independence, its highest level an attenuated needle. As educated Africans spoke the language of nationalism (and, in Tanzania, of socialism as well), they also expected to enjoy the benefits of privilege. Even in Tanzania, the elite maintained its position (130). Oral literature was therefore partially revived to meet the academic cravings of the emergent elites who, though passionate about the academic revival and advancement of the discipline, were for practical considerations, more interested in teaching out of nationalism, grades or publications or all. It would not be kind to rubbish all the effort by these pioneers, but my contention is that as the performances were being recorded for Western Education Standards, effort should have been invested equally in capturing, teaching, and examining African oral literature in its genuine form in the community and not as a derivative. As a result, we got publications and in rare cases, audio tapes but missed out on the vibrant living lore that finds its expression in the intercourse between a charged performance and an equally gratuitous audience. This tradition persists up to today. There is no dialogic engagement between scholars of the living art and their students on one side, and the community of creators, performers, and preservers on the other. The various camps work at cross purposes pursuing different goals.

The "success" of the pioneers, in mounting oral literature as an examinable discipline in schools to universities regrettably, led to complacency among scholars of oral literature at the time and the government of the day. This is confirmed by the decline in broad-based, publicly-funded organized research in Kenyan oral literature from 1980s to 2000. Scholars argued that a lot of material had been collected and what was needed was analysis and not further fieldwork. Methodologically, they were suggesting that data collection and analysis are different research activities that can be handled separately by different people in different locations and epochs. It is appropriate to acknowledge that once the nationalistic favour settled, and the flag of independence confirmed, the government's interest in promoting African culture waned, and with it evaporated the enthusiasm of fieldworkers. Mlama, reflecting on oral performances in Tanzania after independence, posits that "oral poetic genre has been hijacked and manipulated by the political class for the benefit of the ruling classes, leading to its domestication and disempowerment" (24).

Anyumbaism in Kenyan Oral Literature Tradition

It is difficult to discuss the growth of scholarship in Kenyan oral literature without locating the academic footprints of Owuor Anyumba, who made tremendous contribution in the development of fieldwork in oral literature in the country. As mentioned earlier, he was among the eminent scholars that championed the shift from English literature to Literature in English in East Africa. As a scholar of oral literature, first at the Institute of African Studies and later on in the Department of Literature, University of Nairobi, he made tremendous contribution in laying the foundation for systematic oral literature fieldwork in Kenya, and possibly in the East African region. Operating with zeal in the 60s, 70s and 80s, Anyumba recorded several performances based on the structuralist school. Most of the recordings were done with students of the University of Nairobi under his training while the rest he did alone.

As a researcher, Anyumba collected, documented and analysed *nyatiti* praise poems in Luo Nyanza published under the title of *Nyatiti Lament Songs* (1964). Anyumba succumbed to cancer in 1992 without having analysed the massive data he had collected and stored in tapes and interview transcripts. His plan had been to process and publish this material at a later date. He had interest in collection and analysis of texts using structural anthropological methods which entailed looking for patterns, clues, harmony, and cultural belief systems in performances. Masheti Masinjila refers to "Anyumba's dictum" in a discussion of theoretical issues in oral literature in Kenya. He credits Anyumba for laying the foundation for 'structural analysis of oral narratives' by Kenyan researchers (Masinjila, 10). In a preface to Rose Mwangi's *Kikuyu Folktales*, Anyumba advises scholars of oral literature to "attempt to make more comprehensive collections with analyses of motifs, leit-motifs, in the many variant forms" (Mwangi, vii).

The new millennium heralds a new phase in the development of oral literature which is marked by a revival of interest in oral literature scholarship through a multi-disciplinary engagement with historians, anthropologists, philosophers, linguists, medical practitioners, sociologists and economists. There is equal interest in theoretical, technological and methodological issues. Further, scholarship in orality has recognised the centrality of storytellers and performance as integral components in the intellectual enterprise. Scholars have realised that digital society is not a dream but a reality with significant benefits to oral artists, audience, and the society. Oral artists, audience, and scholars are therefore exploring possibilities that exist in taming technology to aid the cultural renaissance sweeping across the villages and the urban centres. Received with resistance initially, there is quick realisation that though digital revolution poses some risks like depersonalisation and invasion of privacy, it still has significant value. The benefits are noted in terms of expanding the audience reach, exposing artists to different cultures and contributing to global understanding. African scholars and practitioners of oral literature are beginning to venture into the cyberspace gradually and reaping enormous benefits socially and financially.

This chapter has raised issues touching on the evolving nature and functions of verbal arts. It confirms that oral literature in Kenya is alive and dynamic. It credits personalities who have made significant contributions to the development of the discipline and highlights its roots in the neighbouring disciplines in social sciences and humanities. What stands out in this chapter is the ability of oral literature to integrate itself into the ever changing environment with considerable ease.

Research in Oral Literature

This chapter focuses on research in African oral literature based on the existing knowledge and the experiences of the author. Research is a systematic process for generating new knowledge or for confirming existing knowledge. It is the exploration for knowledge through objective and systematic methods of finding solutions to a problem. Research involves "deliberate actions in identifying the problem, formulating hypotheses, collecting and analyzing data and reaching certain conclusions either in the form of solution(s) towards the concerned problem or in certain generalizations for some theoretical formulation" (Kothari, 2). Research, for that reason, is a disciplined quest for knowledge with a clear roadmap regardless of the disciplinary home of the study be it Anthropology, Linguistics, Literature or Aviation Electronics. Researchers rely mainly on primary and secondary data to address research questions. Primary data is that which is collected afresh for the first time, and as a consequence should be original in character, while secondary data is that which has already been collected, analysed, interpreted and packaged in a certain form by someone else. Research that relies mainly on secondary data is documentary by nature and as a rule is found in libraries and archives, whereas a study that sets out to capture and analyse primary data is field-based. It should be mentioned early enough that in orate societies where court poets were employed by the leadership to keep the history of society alive and relevant, such living libraries and archives were repositories of secondary data which had been collected and stored for posterity. They are good examples of living archives.

Oral literature is a performance based discipline. It is inconceivable to discuss oral literature without addressing its performative aspects. Research in oral literature is essentially field-based. Only supplementary information is generated from secondary sources. Field research is therefore, "the study of people working in the natural courses of their daily lives" (Emerson, 1). A field worker, as enunciated by Emerson, ventures into the worlds of others in order to learn first-hand about how they live, how they perform and react to their own oral literature, and what captivates and distresses them. Generally, the main aim of research is to find out the truth which has not been discovered as yet or to verify what is assumed to be the existing knowledge.

Qualitative and Quantitative Research Methods

Research can be qualitative, quantitative or both. The word "qualitative" implies an emphasis on the qualities of entities and on processes and meanings that are not experimentally examined. Qualitative researchers stress the socially constructed nature of reality, the intimate relationship between the researcher and what is studied, and the situational constraints that shape a given inquiry. Such researchers emphasise the value-laden nature of inquiry. They seek answers 'to questions that stress how social experience is created and given meaning (Denzin and Lincoln, 8). The method developed from a phenomenological perspective following the writings of Max Weber. A German sociologist and political economist, Weber was a respected pioneer in interpretive sociology. He sought to understand meaning of action from the perspective of those involved. The motivation of a researcher to employ this approach was derived from the *Verstehen* tradition, a German word for empathy:

> The scientist who engages in verstehen tries to make empathetic sense of the phenomenon by looking for the perspective from which the phenomenon appears to be meaningful and appropriate. ... After all, the only way to acquire scientifically respectable knowledge of a phenomenon is to gain comprehensive insight into what is of crucial importance to the essence of the phenomenon; in the case of the mental phenomena, this means grasping their meaning. (Smelser & Baltes, 16165)

The *verstehen* tradition demands of researchers to put themselves into the place of the subject of inquiry to gain understanding of the others' view of reality, of their symbols, values and attitudes, and ultimately, meaning. Qualitative research is, therefore, likely to provide a deeper understanding of the oral literature texts performed at the community level.

"Quantitative" study, alternatively, is premised on the idea that social phenomenon is quantified, measured and expressed numerically in terms that can be analyzed using statistical methods. It emphasises the measurement and analysis of causal relationships between variables and not processes. Proponents of quantitative studies claim that their work is done from within a value-free framework. Previously, researchers subscribing to either of the two schools spent their valuable time competing for 'scientific' superiority with quantitative researchers dismissing qualitative school as impressionistic and too subjective for scientific verification. Qualitative researchers often responded by insisting that they are humanists interested in the total environment of the subject of study instead of mechanical fixation with figures, tables, percentages and frequencies. They berated quantitative researchers as mechanical, de-humanised and removed from the reality they claim to interpret.

The truth of the matter is that, there is no research that is purely quantitative or exclusively qualitative. Even oral literature research, originally deemed to be purely qualitative, requires some elements of quantitative methods of inquiry. In stressing the importance of blending the two seemingly antagonistic approaches, I argue that our interest as researchers, should not so much be a question of which paradigm we belong to, but how to dissolve the imaginary methodological boundaries between the two camps in the interest of research designs that serve the investigation at hand without self-imposed restrictions. Both quantitative and qualitative research methods are and can be used complimentarily. A nuanced application of both methods can yield deeper insights about the situation studied without compromising the integrity of the process or results.

Demystifying Fieldwork

Young researchers have often approached fieldwork as an obscure area of scholarship that requires only the highly gifted individuals. While this is a fact, it should not be used to mystify the practice of disciplined quest. The fact of the matter is that in everyday life we are all fieldworkers differing in degrees of commitment, ideological and theoretical grounding. Our everyday pattern of life reflects all the major skills of fieldwork, which include participating genuinely, looking keenly, listening attentively, collecting meticulously, questioning radically, and interpreting with an open mind. For example, a farmer planting two kinds of maize seeds side by side to evaluate yields, a herbalist sequencing two concoctions based on their toxicities, a pastor assessing her congregation in terms of size, gender, age, career against the volume of tithe received and a sociologist questioning villagers about their feelings towards family planning are all doing research.

We are, perhaps, rarely aware that the very act of living is a manifestation of field working. There are different, and at times competing, definitions of fieldwork in oral literature. The weight tends to lean on the disciplinary background of the researcher. As mentioned earlier, oral literature is a borderline discipline that accommodates fieldworkers with different and at times even competing interests. The matter is further complicated by the fact that oral literature cuts across history, religious studies, philosophy, linguistics, anthropology, sociology and literature. These are academic siblings that have not forgotten their childhood differences even in their old age. Kothari correctly points out that 'regardless of the discipline involved, research, is a process of purposeful, in-depth investigation of a particular issue which follows a defined structured approach to obtain answers that generate understanding and greater awareness of an idea, thereby achieving additional knowledge and meaning' (7).

Fieldworkers who live, observe, and describe the daily lives, behaviours; languages and performances of a group of people over a given period are ethnographers. Oral literature research therefore falls partially under ethnographic research tradition since, as Finnegan notes, 'the sequence of intellectual fashions is ultimately no different in the study of oral arts and traditions from that in any other sphere of anthropological study' (Finnegan, 27). Yet most of the publications emanating from research in oral literature remain ethnographic at the ethnic level without providing a broader comparative scope the globalizing world needs. Kaschula (2001) in calling for new ethnography urges researchers to go beyond fixation with what I call "ethnic oral literatures" of individual societies to more composite oral literatures that accept ethnic oral literatures but as part of the national, regional, continental and ultimately global oral literature:

> There is need for this ethnography to move between the micro and macro aspects of our society. For example, the West African griot can be studied ethnographically in a Senegalese or Mali village. Equally so, the work of a griot or musician, Salief Keita, should be studied in relation to his contribution to global literature. An

awareness of ethnography in relation to both national and global
culture may become increasingly necessary, giving rise to a new
type of ethnography. (xiii)

Whereas globalization of oral literatures through research that
Kaschula proposes is commendable in a society that is shrinking
by the day, it should not be done at the expense of retaining
cultural peculiarities of the source communities that create,
consume and preserve verbal arts. It is equally important that
fieldworkers remain cautious and focused when using
ethnographic research methods in investigating oral literature
research problems because such fieldworkers are not trained
ethnographers, neither are their goals similar to those of
traditional ethnographers. What unites the two is the
methodology of entering the community, conducting
investigations and analyzing data to reach certain conclusions. It
is easier for cultural anthropologists conducting research in oral
literature to employ ethnographic research methods competently
based on their training. This does not mean that they may
perform better than fellow researchers with literary background.
Each one of them must make adjustments to cover the aspects
they are not conversant with. The two groups have the potential
to complement each other in their scholarly pursuits and should
work in partnership.

Multidisciplinarity in Oral Literature

Oral literature in its nature and function is multidisciplinary.
These disciplines co-exist in close neighbourhoods because, like
living organisms, they share characteristics: grow, change and

converge. Continuous mutation, convergence and divergence of disciplines problematizes any rigid genre demarcation since they flow into each other with ease, form and deform with time. Terry Eagleton (1978), a theoretician, captures this fluidity in literature thus: "a piece of work may start off life as history or philosophy and then come to be ranked as literature or it may start off as literature and then come to be valued for its archaeological significance. Some texts are born literature, some achieve literariness, and some have literariness thrust upon them" (8). Belief in the social construction of knowledge through collaboration in collecting, analyzing and reporting fieldwork is the foundation of oral literature research. The place of the study of oral literature in the hierarchy of knowledge belongs both 'to humanities and to social sciences' because oral literature, as a genre of folklore, is a borderline discipline, which can only exist in a multidisciplinary environment (Botkin, 199).

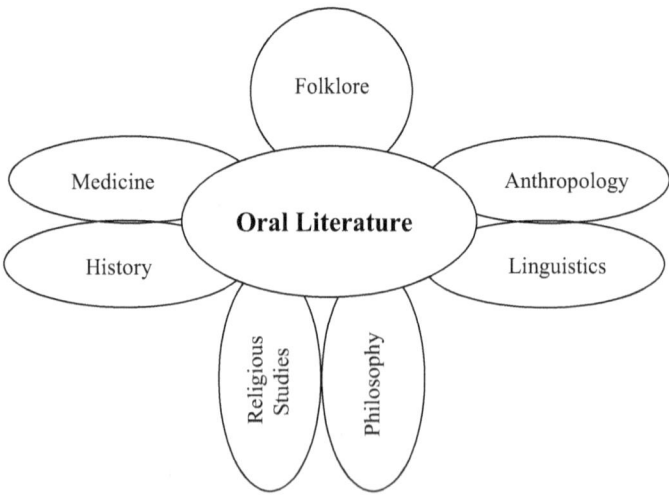

Figure 1: The multidisciplinary nature of oral literature

As the diagram above shows, it is quite challenging to fence off oral literature away from the neighbouring disciplines in natural sciences, social sciences, and humanities without stifling its development. Indeed, oral literature is the bridge that links humanities to social and natural sciences. Linguists, ethnologists and anthropologists, for example, were among the first scholars to notice the value of oral literature to their disciplines. All the related disciplines are, therefore, legitimate stakeholders in oral literature scholarship. For example, theologians approach oral literature with a religious slant, sociologists give it a sociological angle, linguists look at it from their background while literature scholars give it a performance approach. I advance the view that oral literature, by its very nature, is open to multi-disciplinary investigation which makes various approaches from the disciplinary divide not only acceptable but also desirable. Oral literature fieldworkers benefit more if they come out of their disciplinary backyards to embrace what other neighbouring disciplines contribute to orality. In the same vein, scholars in humanities, social sciences and 'hard' sciences benefit more in their interactions with communities when they embrace ethnographic research methods in their work.

Fieldwork Defined

I find it safe to treat fieldwork in oral literature as "an exploratory and an analytical activity, planned and implemented by an oral literature student in locations which are not under the jurisdiction of the university or the sponsoring research institution, with the main purpose of contributing to knowledge in the discipline both quantitatively and qualitatively." I have used 'student' in the definition in a broader sense deliberately to refer to all participants in oral literature fieldwork since they remain students of the cultures they study regardless of their educational backgrounds, social and professional status. I also deliberately mention who should conduct research in oral literature to control misguided adventurism that characterised early studies by missionaries, explorers and tourists to Africa and other parts of the world considered backward. Fieldwork does not include activities officially undertaken by research students outside the academic domain. Trips by university students to participate in sporting events, funerals, political rallies, picnics and tours do not qualify to be considered as fieldwork. It is important to make this distinction clear because it determines the formulation of research methodology at the level of planning, field discipline, budget allocation and the expected deliverables at the end of the activity.

Does it then imply that opportunistic cases cannot be exploited by a fieldworker? That is not the case. I advance the position that for fieldwork to be conducted judiciously there should be a research methodology. Unplanned opportunities for mining data should be accommodated within the methodology. There are studies that may rely entirely on unplanned performances. Good examples in African oral literature include fieldwork on dirges or proverbs. A fieldworker cannot wish or predict death in a community to collect poetry of loss and hope. Proverbs too come out at those inspired moments in a conversation or disputation; they are never planned. They come out only when an occasion demands it and a wise man or woman is around to employ them to spice up the conversation and communicate the collective philosophy of the society.

I normally read in the faces of my undergraduate students on the first lecture on fieldwork methodology that, apart from mundane academic considerations, they join the course believing that it promises an exciting picnic. This cannot be denied. Westernisation of education in Africa made learning boring by shifting it to the confines of four walls in schools, colleges and universities. Learning from "the people's university", that is the village or community was discouraged. University students therefore look forward to field trips, not as opportunities for learning from the people, but as an escape from the rigid confines of the lecture halls. However, although it incorporates an element of expedition, fieldwork cannot be reduced to aimless adventure. In the past, my undergraduate class would normally start off at the beginning of the semester with a handful of students. The class would then increase gradually and finally overflow as the day of fieldwork trip approached. Initially I would be bothered that the late-comers wanted to participate in fieldwork without attending the requisite number of lecture hours for a thorough grounding in methodology. Only later did I realise that these were joy riders whose main interest was 'to be out there.'

Once the class returned to the campus from fieldwork such students disappeared into thin air without giving any explanation or submitting their fieldwork reports. Such activities disgrace fieldwork. I have been disappointed to learn that in some disciplines joyriding during fieldwork is the norm rather than the exception. These adventure-loving students are allowed to pay up to travel with bonafide fieldworkers to the research site. Such students go to the field without any academic agenda, apart from overindulging in merriment and exhibitionist tendencies. At best, fieldwork joy riders are a liability that any lead researcher should not entertain. They take up space in the transport facility, are generally uninterested in research methodology and are therefore idle, rowdy, and bad influence in the field. In addition, this unnecessary baggage causes overcrowding in the field and dissipates the energy of the lead researcher by distracting him or her from managing the data collection activity to concentrate on crowd control and *ad hoc* disciplinary meetings. I am not suggesting that fieldworkers should not enjoy themselves while they are 'out there.' Fieldwork can be dull without some exciting interludes, but everything must be done within the margins of guided scholarship.

Fieldwork in oral literature is a collaborative exercise. Collaboration should not be limited to the communities studied. As mentioned earlier, it begins with methodological collaboration with the disciplines that neighbour it. Collaboration is methodologically consistent with ethnographers' belief in the social construction of knowledge. It calls for shared methods for collecting, analyzing and reporting fieldwork (Horner, 17). Oral literature fieldworkers should empathetically connect with communities studied. They have to "step out' to adopt outsiders' perspective when investigating unfamiliar (or even familiar) patterns, attempting to penetrate or unveil the many layers of behaviours and beliefs that make people think and act as they do (Chiseri-Strater, E & B.S. Sunstein 7). Most important, the connection must be two-way. Fieldworkers must create environments that enable source communities to engage constructively with researchers as agents and not mere data mines.

To engage with host communities constructively, fieldworkers must humanise the myth of objectivity in research. Even though fieldwork is crucial, the field is imagined as untouched by the researcher's work. The researcher is assumed to observe the field from a privileged location of "detached impartiality" above the field, his observations having no impact on, while accurately identifying truths of, the field (Horner, 15).

Fieldworkers, contrary to this assumption, do not depend on detachment or on the objectivity that comes from stepping out of a culture. They rely on human involvement – their gut reactions or subjective responses to cultural practices. Fieldwork in oral literature is primarily subjective. It is not always objectivity or detachment that allows us to study culture, whether our own or others. Subjectivity allows us to uncover some features of culture that are not always apparent. Distanced and objective stance in fieldwork is dishonest because to ignore yourself as part of data distorts your findings. We have to remember that as fieldworkers we literally select particular details, record informant's voices, choose what to retain and what to remove, and decide how to write about the particular as it illuminates the human condition studied.

The term field is perceived differently by students of oral literature. I have had opportunity to conduct research near the

University of Nairobi which is located in the heart of Nairobi, the capital city of Kenya. Similarly, I have done a lot of field research in locations far away in the remote parts of the country and abroad. Young field workers oftentimes consider the 'field' to be a location far away from the university or research institution, possibly in far-flung villages on top of steep mountains or deep down in the valleys untouched by the craze of modernity. Such students are less enthusiastic to enrol in oral literature class if the 'field' is a slum on the fringes of the city, or affluent estates in the leafy suburbs of the city. This limitation in the understanding of 'the field' afflicts many researchers. They are trapped in the ideology of British social anthropology at the beginning of the 20thCentury that believed that anthropology was about studying the 'primitive other' in the colonised frontiers in Africa and Asia. I do not subscribe to the narrow and selective definition of the field for oral literature research. I hold the view that oral literature research can be carried out successfully both in the neighbourhood of a university situated in the city like the University of Nairobi in Kenya or Hamburg University in Germany or any city anywhere in the world, just as it is done in the villages in the developing parts of the world.

In modern times, there has been intense debate among scholars and researchers of oral literature in Kenya on the ideal location for oral literature fieldwork. Two schools have emerged which I prefer to call the 'conservative school' and the 'modernist school'. The 'conservative school' believes that traditional forms of performances should be preserved in their 'authentic' forms as part of the intangible heritage of a community. Advocates of the school further argue that modernity has interfered with the traditional village life and diluted oral performances, hence the need to conduct fieldwork in remote rural villages where unadulterated traditional performances still exist.

One of the scholars who represent this thinking is Njoroge Ngugi who refers to "the village oral literature" popularised by Okot p'Bitek, as "the real thing" (49). By implication, this school suggests that modernity is at war with the traditional cultures and that, indeed, it is winning thus the justification to fortify culturally virgin villages. This school is driven by the belief in an oral literature canon. The great tradition in oral literature, according to this school, lies in the original, pure, unadulterated performances in remote villages. The school has not addressed clearly what it means by "authentic" African oral literature.

The opposing school of 'modernists' believe that society is dynamic and so its verbal art. Modernisation together with the rise in cosmopolitan culture leads to the emergence of new forms of oral literature that are neither modern nor purely traditional but a blend of the new and the old. This type of oral literature can only be found in urban environments. Modernists dismiss the conservative school arguing that by concentrating on research in remote parts of the country, such scholars perpetuate the "deep-bush fallacy." The myth is premised on the assumption that oral literature is a quaint art only found among those left behind by economic development.

Both camps miss the point because of their exclusivist approach to oral literature fieldwork. No serious scholar of oral literature can ignore emerging forms of performances in towns and cities, especially at a time when professional artists are migrating from impoverished villages in the countryside to urban centres in search of exposure, enabling infrastructure, cosmopolitan audience, and better remuneration. At the same time, there is formidable evidence that context shapes oral performances. Communities that have remained loyal to their traditional beliefs and practices like the Turkana, Pokot, Borana, and Maasai of Kenya tend to have rich performances that reflect the resilience of their culture in a changing society. Having conducted fieldwork in urban slums of the city of Nairobi, Kenya and in Seoul, South Korea, and remote villages in rural Kenya, I have learnt that there is nothing purely traditional or truly urban in oral performances. What shapes performances are the artists, audience, and performance atmosphere. This provides ground for treating urban and rural oral literatures as two sides of the same coin. The common factor in both traditional and modern oral literatures is that they are all subject to change and may completely be different from what they are in the coming decades. The Department of Literature at the University of Nairobi has four oral literature field sites which cover both urban and rural settings. The selection was based on cultural diversity, geographical representation and way of life of the people studied. The fieldwork research stations are in Kwale District in Coast Province (Urban/rural setting), Samburu District in Rift Valley province (urban/rural setting), Kiboswa cluster on the boundaries of Nyanza, Western and Rift Valley Provinces (rural setting) and Kibera slums in the city of Nairobi (Urban slum setting).

Students from the Department of Literature conducting fieldwork in Golini, Kwale District, one of the research stations of the University of Nairobi, July 2008. *Picture by Peter Wasamba*

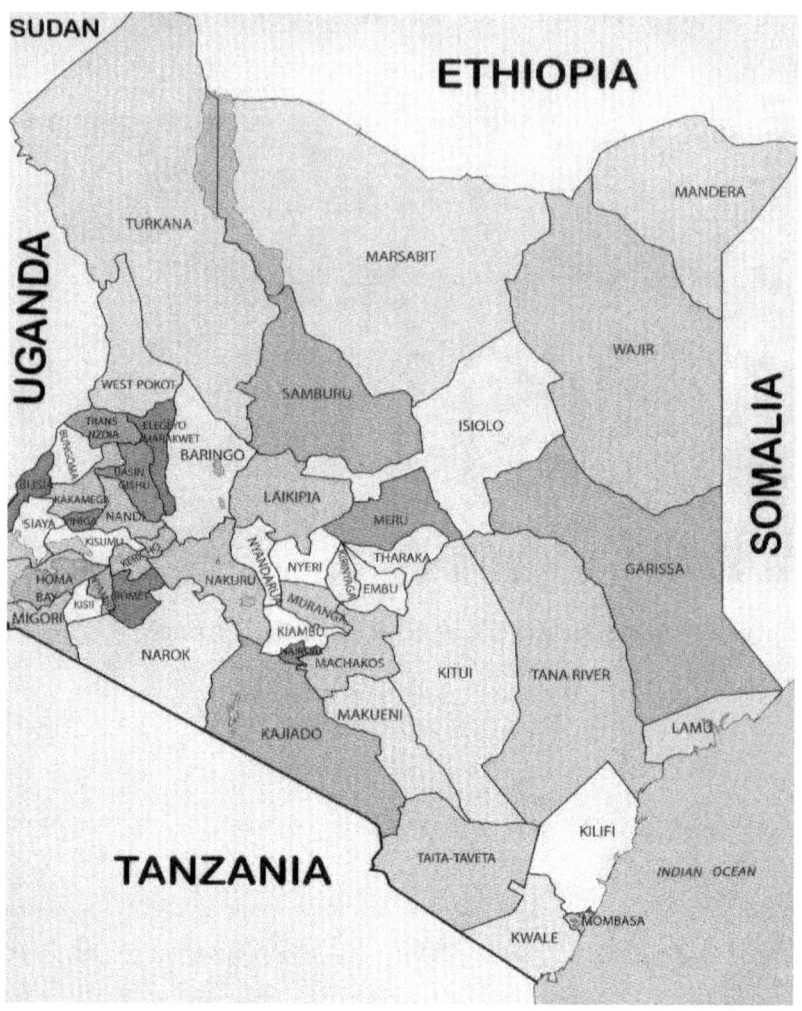

Map of Kenya indicating research sites

Responsibilities of a Fieldworker

An oral literature fieldworker has five key interrelated responsibilities. Failure to perform one effectively affects others as well. Even though fieldworkers are people who are hardly found in their offices, they do more than just going to the field to collect materials. A good fieldworker is: a good collector, a thorough analyst of data collected, a superb teacher, a good disseminator of research information through publications and a professional administrator. A fieldworker must get out and come to grips with the raw data, as it exists out there in terms of who performs what, where, when, with whom and with what effect? Following data collection, a fieldworker settles on that data for interpretation. We always go to the field expecting some results. Interpreting data enables us to find out if the study has yielded what we observed in the field or something contrary. The third phase deals with dissemination of the fieldwork findings through printed, filmed, or recorded products. This is followed by the preservation of the discipline by teaching it to others and archiving the collected material for reference.

Thorough teaching requires the courage to learn alongside students, passion and patience, and the hope that students will reflect on their lives through the process of field working. If one happens to be a good teacher in class, it is partly because they have been able, not only to give their students fresh knowledge from the field, but also to light in their minds and hearts, fire for systematic inquiry through field working. Finally, there is office work and administration, where one accomplishes all the things that have to be done to get other parts of the work underway.

The current thinking is that a fieldworker should not stop at administration but also venture into intervention. I have argued before that fieldwork is subjective and mostly driven by empathy. It cannot therefore be justifiable that researchers visit communities in dire need of intervention but assume that they are constrained by ethics of research from doing so. There is need to include intervention on behalf of the respondents in the fieldwork methodology. This is a contentious proposal that is likely to attract support from civil society and faith-based organizations, but generate disapproval from career fieldworkers and research funders, who believe that fieldwork as a science is different from intervention associated with the non-governmental organisations (NGOs) and governmental agencies. I see researchers losing the battle to hold themselves apart from what affects societies they deeply depend on to conduct their studies. It is just a matter of time.

Fieldworkers cannot be immune to the plight of the communities they are working with. At the same time, they cannot abandon research to be fully engaged in meeting the immediate needs of the host community. As mentioned earlier on, what a good fieldworker needs is good judgment and balance. In 2003, while collecting oral narratives among the Digo of Vuga in Kwale, one day at about 11:00am, the performance became ecstatic very quickly. The drumming, singing, chants and dancing climaxed into a spectacular display of exquisite moves by the audience. Within a short time, young people started streaming into the area from the narrow footpaths connecting the adjoining homes. Suddenly, the homestead was full of dancers and chorus. What shocked me was that eighty per-cent of the audience comprised children below thirteen years old, yet it was a school day. Most of these dancers were children of oral artists. It made me understand why chronic poverty in oral artist-headed households in the area was contagious. We spared sometime after the performances to explore why children were not in school and learnt that poverty, illiteracy among parents, the lure of making easy money at the beach for girls, prospects of early marriages and many school levies had made it impossible for children, especially young girls to go to school. A visit to the District Education officer confirmed that Kwale was among the poor performing districts in the Kenya Certificate for Primary Examinations (KCPE). It had been performing poorly for years. We discussed ways in which community initiatives, efforts of governmental and non-governmental organizations can be harnessed to promote education in the locality. Apart from data collection, we participated quietly in a campaign to promote children's education in the area. This is an example of a modest intervention fieldworkers can make without abandoning their fieldwork mandate.

Oral Literature and Globalization

Fieldwork in oral literature is expensive in terms of time, risks, resources and expectations of the fieldworker, the subjects of the study, the sponsoring institution and other participants. It cannot be purposeless. In deed, fieldwork is key to the survival, growth, and the preservation of the priceless intangible heritage. In the era of globalisation, it is often assumed that oral literature in Africa has no place due to craze for European, American, and Asian cultures. It is further believed, erroneously so, that globalisation is only about international trade. What has not been accepted by African bureaucrats is that globalisation, first and foremost, opens up a market for cultures. As people take their goods and services to other regions, their cultures precede the merchandise. This explains why many western embassies in African capital cities have vibrant Culture and Information sections. One may ask: 'what are Africans taking to the global cultural market?' Even what is genuinely African like tea and coffee are processed and given brand names that market cultures alien to Africa. Consequently, the young generation is confused and live in a dream world where the ability to discard African values for the inferior and ill-suited exotic cultures is a badge of 'civilization'.

This cultural rootlessness is succinctly captured by Taban lo Liyong (1990) in *Another Last Word* where he laments that "Our past has been so grossly ridiculed, so systematically eliminated, that we have grown up with phobia about our past so that we look rootless or are actually rootless" (Liyong, 72). The foregoing discussion illuminates the importance of oral literature research in our institutions of learning.

Importance of Fieldwork

Existence of oral literature outside fieldwork is unimaginable. It is through field exposure that the researcher acquires a deeper insight into the verbal art of a given community. Fieldwork in oral literature builds bridges between communities, families, learning institutions, and students. It fosters and enriches our respect and appreciation for who we are and how we are connected to the larger community. Further, through fieldwork, we gain respect and appreciation for those groups or individuals who are "different" from ourselves; preserve the cultures of our various African communities, and reveal a powerful expression of resilient community spirit. In addition, fieldwork enables practitioners to gain a better understanding of the techniques and functions of verbal art. The very fact that schools, colleges, universities, research institutions, and UN agencies like UNESCO and WIPO support activities related to verbal art confirms the respect the discipline continues to command in modern society both locally and globally.

Fieldwork in oral literature gives students opportunity to update and apply skills in the use of research equipment. This point may sound frivolous because it is unbelievable that a university student or graduate should fail the test of operating a voice recorder in the field. Though voice recorders are available locally, they are hardly considered as research equipment; they are only played for entertainment. It is for this reason that students normally have problems in using basic recording machines for fieldwork. The problem is compounded when students opt for digital recording equipment. To this extent, it can be safely argued that field research provides opportunity for students to refine their skills in the use of research equipment. I remember an incident in 2005 when the Kenya Oral Literature Association (KOLA) organised a refresher course for all lecturers of oral literature in Kenyan universities, both public and private. The event, which took place in the coastal city of Mombasa, addressed theories in oral literature, fieldwork methodology, and practicals in interviewing and recording. During fieldwork, we noticed that there were lecturers who had problems operating their voice recording machines. This embarrassing situation was not because of the scholars' ineptitude, but low frequency in the use of the equipment in a scientific environment. This anecdote emphasises the need to conduct fieldwork regularly using up-to-date machines to master their use. In some embarrassing cases, researchers record interviews using digital equipment but cannot retrieve the data due to the file format conflict.

Whereas there has been enthusiasm and urgency in collecting African oral performances, the agenda has been driven by different ideological, political, pedagogical and literary interests. A number of scholars have supported research in African oral literature out of genuine concern that these treasured cultural expressions of communities' intangible heritage are quickly fading away, and that if not preserved, they may never be accessed by future generations. This school argues that traditional stories and songs should be put down in print, not so much for the investigator's own purposes, but for "future generations" or young and new members of the society. They argue that indigenous cultures are dying, that the printed word must replace the spoken one if there is to be any hope of continuance, and that except for the efforts of the investigator, the oral traditions of one native community or another would be lost forever. Naomi Kipury (1983), Kavetsa Adagala and Wanjiku Kabira (1985) and Wanjiku Kabira and Karega Mutahi (1988), share this position. Writing on the *Enanga* praise poets of the Bahaya of Tanzania, Mulokozi similarly elucidates this argument with more persuasive power. He notes that the status of *enanga* bards has changed tremendously since independence, particularly after the post-independence abolition of kingship among the Bahaya:

> Many performing bards are old and poor. (In my research in 1979, I discovered that more than 50 percent are above 50 years old, and more than 90 percent are above 35 years. There was no bard below 25 years.) The more enterprising perform for money but are not, strictly speaking, professionals, since they depend on agriculture for their basic subsistence. New people, youths, are not joining the profession. It follows, therefore, that the enanga epic poetry is withering away and, if the present trend continues, will disappear completely in the next fifty years. (Mulokozi, 284)

Not all researchers subscribe to the theory of the eminent death of African oral literature. Johnson William John in *heelloy: Modern Poetry and Songs of the Somali* (1986) correctly observes that there is a general fear that the traditional Somali poetry is dying. This fear is poignant in the elite. The fear has led to a frantic scramble to record as much traditional poetry as possible before the genre dies. Johnson calls this fear of 'death' of the genre and the attendant mad rash to document for preservation a "misunderstanding into the nature of Somali oral poetry":

> The so-called death may be characteristic of the oral process itself. Something had to preced the gabay, from which the gabay could develop. Culture and its characteristic attributes are dynamic and in a constant state of flux. If traditional poetry is dying... one thing remains absolutely certain: the art of composing oral poetry in Somalia is not about to die. If a specific poem, or even a genre, does die, the art of oral poetry goes on, and indeed is enjoying a

renaissance today with the revival and development of the modern
poem. (16)

Johnson speaks for the category of researchers who are guided by
dynamism in oral art and the continuous renewal of the genre.
He is in sync with Russel Kaschula (2001) who is categorical that
the death of oral literature is out of question: "The only question
that begs further research is: how is oral literature adapting and
functioning within the modern world?" (xii). This group of
fieldworkers have explained their involvement in oral literature
fieldwork on the need to continually study the changing nature
of a genre that many admit is highly fluid. They are interested in
theories and methods employed in the collection and analysis of
performances and strongly believe that oral literature lives
because of its dynamism, adaptability and relevance to the
changing society.

Whereas the motive of the preservation school sounds
compelling, scrutiny of the research by scholars advocating for
'preservation before loss' indicates that majority are not
contemporary career oral literature fieldworkers. They collected
oral literature material in the '70s and '80s either to meet the
requirements of their university degrees or for book publication
to aid in the teaching of the discipline in schools and colleges.
These scholars concentrated on fieldwork in their communities
with little or no comparison with neighbouring communities.
This has led to the phenomenon of ethnic oral literatures in
Kenya. To date, there is no text that reflects vividly the collage
of the Kenyan cultural diversity, yet communities manifest
cultural eclecticism and convergence in many aspects. To an

extent, it can be argued that violent ethnic conflict that flared up in Kenya immediately after the disputed presidential election results of December 2007 confirmed the failure of oral literature scholars to bridge the divide between various Kenyan ethnic cultures. The void was filled by politicians who massaged ethnic differences to create safe colonies of ethnic voters turned hate-mongers, arsonists and murderers. The result was catastrophic as Kenyans became sadists immune to the suffering of other communities.

I subscribe to the school of oral literature fieldworkers who approach the discipline as an enduring art and not a dying genre. This is simply because so long as human communities have the power of speech and the capacity to imagine and share their mental pictures through verbal creative expressions, there will always be oral literature. The earlier assumptions that oral forms were 'dying out' and needed salvaging are being contested for both intellectual reasons and for impliedly freezing supposed 'older' forms as if in a museum (Finnegan 217). It is for this reason that Taban lo Liyong (1990) is correct in asserting that "Oral literature never dies" (71).

Fieldwork enhances the capacity of community members as performers, researchers and analysts of their own art. In the recent past, research as a profession was detached from the people and shrouded in mystery. It was considered an activity that requires very educated people from outside the community, in some cases, even from outside the continent of Africa. Early fieldworkers in Africa who were mostly European missionaries, explorers, and ethnologists promoted this myth. They were detached from local communities culturally, linguistically, and intellectually. When their time was up, they handed the myth of mystery in fieldwork to African elite who inherited and perpetuated it for self interest. The gap between host communities and fieldworkers consequently created ignorance, resentment, and detachment in host communities. The myth of a researcher being a mystic still persists today in some Kenyan communities and research institutions. This disconnect has contributed greatly to research fatigue or unreasonable demands for fees which often compromises quality in research activities. Recent trends, however, indicate the narrowing of the gap between fieldworkers and community members. I have since learned that even villagers who may not have formal education are good researchers. A successful oral literature fieldwork should tap and enhance the neglected indigenous resources of local people as artists, critics and researchers because members of host communities participate effectively in the research process as performers, guides, informants, evaluators and consumers of the research product. Such involvement can demystify fieldwork and make it an ongoing activity at the community level long after the researcher has left the field.

In 2006, while conducting research among the Terrik community of Kapsengere along the border of Nyanza, Western and Rift Valley provinces in Kenya, the community leaders stubbornly denied me opportunity to record their poetic and narrative genres. The reason advanced was that community elders did not want their traditional knowledge given away to strangers who may distort it for other interests including financial gain. Conscious of ethics governing informed consent, I was disappointed but also happy at the same time; disappointed that I had been blocked from recording performances assured are rich in folk knowledge, but encouraged that there are communities acutely conscious of their intellectual property rights over folklore that no researcher can access it without negotiating for permission. Later, I was shocked to learn that I had been blocked from documenting the performances because the community allegedly has some arrangements with Japanese researchers who also collect data in the same location. I was further told that the stubborn gate-keepers who ensure local researchers do not operate in the area had benefitted from a trip to Japan. For the first time, I realised that corruption has not spared field working.

I wondered why a community would block local scholars from conducting research in a Kenyan village but welcome people from other continents ready to part with attractive incentives. The scope of this book does not allow us to explore what happens in the mind of villagers especially when they meet two fieldworkers: one ready to reward them handsomely but does not respect their culture and the other well meaning but not materially endowed. Chances are that they will perform for the rich and send the well-meaning researcher away due to pecuniary reasons. I had to decide whether to forego data collection because of community elders who had been compromised by foreign researchers or use other creative ways to document performances. I discovered a way out. Informal discussions with a few young men revealed that they were not happy with the way elders were treating us. They did not agree with the elders' reasoning that custom did not allow for recording of their performances. We took advantage of the goodwill from the youth who, after being

assured that the recording would be done far from the elders'
office, agreed to be interviewed. I recorded a few performances,
but the experience was not generally encouraging. Throughout
the performances, I was like a thief, looking at the gate in short
intervals to see if the elders had found us out. Luckily enough,
that never happened and we completed the recording and quietly
walked away to our next interview in a neighbouring
community. I did not like the experience. The guilt that I had
done something wrong kept on gnawing at my conscience. I tried
to moralise over my decision to employ covert means to get data,
but I was still not cured of the feeling that I had stolen from the
community even after being warned.

A lot has been written about the role oral literature fieldwork
plays in filling up gaps in knowledge and verifying existing texts.
These academic aspects of research have been amplified at the
expense of social concerns that go a long with ethnographic
research. In a number of research visits I have conducted in rural
and urban communities in Kenya, I have noted that the decline
in the popularity of oral literature in the contemporary society is
occasioned by the ever-widening gaps between the oral artist, the
audience, and the scholar/researcher. The oral artist is deemed to
be traditional and therefore quaint, the audience is perceived to
be unreliable, sophisticated, and too demanding while the
scholar/researcher is dismissed as a tourist, detached, verbose,
and corrupt. This creates a disjointed triangle in oral literature
composition, performance, and scholarship, which in turn, dilutes
the transactional nature of the art. In this environment, a
researcher is supposed to build bridges of understanding to ensure
harmony between the artist, the community and the researcher.

A successful fieldwork should therefore complete the circle of understanding between oral artists, communities, and fieldworkers to restore trust, promote ownership and reduce the cost of research. Field research in oral literature can be a way of identifying with and understanding the oral artists and the community under the study. Research should assure community members that oral texts are still relevant and useful.

Critical Ethnography

I have learnt in my experiences that, oral literature, by employing the tools of critical ethnography in fieldwork, bridges the gap between oral artists, communities, and scholars by promoting a dialogic learning process akin to the Frerian model of education for empowerment. Critical ethnography emerges from an extensive body of work in critical pedagogy in which the goal of teaching is to engage the students or other groups of learners in the dialogic work of understanding their social location and developing cultural actions appropriate to that location (Brooke and Hogg, 161). Unlike traditional oral literature fieldwork practice, critical ethnography shifts the goal of praxis away from the acquisition of knowledge about the 'other' to the formation of a dialogic relationship with the 'other' whose destination is the social transformation of material conditions that immediately oppress, marginalize, or otherwise subjugate the ethnographic participant. Brown and Sidney observe that this reconfigured praxis seeks to actualize both aspects of the Frerian educational dialectic, in which critical analysis of localized and politicized problem is but a springboard into meaningful action to mitigate, or eliminate those problems (5).

The congruence between critical ethnography and Paulo Freire's pedagogy is that in both approaches, the fieldworker and respondents become learners in the research enterprise. Paraphrasing Freire, one can argue that a conscientizing and therefore liberating oral literature fieldwork is not mere siphoning of verbal arts from respondents deemed to be ignorant of their conditions, it is a true act of learning. Through fieldwork, both the fieldworker and the community simultaneously become knowing subjects, brought together by the object they are studying. There is no longer one who thinks, who knows, standing in front of others who admit they do not know, that they have to be taught. Rather all of them are inquisitive learners, eager to learn. Where participatory fieldwork has taken place, there is conscientization which broadens local people's critical faculties.

Field research in oral literature becomes a way of identifying with and understanding the community under the study. There is 'consciousness-raising in the sense of developing self-critical and self-conscious outlook of members of communities and providing chance for learning from experience' (Freire, 2). It is nevertheless important to point out that researchers should be careful not to shift focus from research in to outright activism on behalf of the host communities because it may make their findings doubtful due to partisanship.

Fieldwork allows students to be more involved in the research process. Instead of leading sedentary lives in libraries and lecture rooms, students who work in field sites and archives learn to observe, listen, interpret, and analyze the behaviours and language of others around them. Fieldwork also exposes students to cultures different from their own through actual contact in their research projects in addition to reading about those cultures. Further, conducting fieldwork encourages understanding of self as each student reads, writes, researches, and reflects on relationships with others. In the course of fieldwork, students become better researchers and writers. It is for this reason that Hawes advises young researchers to, "get out there and do some good hard fieldwork. That is where all your best ideas and your most important knowledge are waiting for you. If you do your work well, folks will teach you back" (73).

Proschan, invoking humanism in ethnographic researchers explains that by virtue of fieldworkers' broad interdisciplinary training and indeed, because of the very nature of the expressive phenomena they study, researchers possess unique abilities to intercede humanely in social and personal crises and to mitigate harmful consequences of social disruption – abilities that impose upon them attendant responsibilities (150). He goes on to assert that 'Knowing our assumptions and recognizing our stereotypes enables us to develop tolerance and respect for customs and groups different from ours because our training and experiences sensitize us to matters of impersonal and inter-ethnic communication to which most people are oblivious' (154). Fieldwork in oral literature, in addition, encourages recontextualization, which entails grounding representations to new audiences in the modes of presentation occurring in a natural context. Recontextualization through field research and scholarship in oral literature makes tradition to be understood as "part of modernity rather than a part of it" (Baron and Spitzer, ix).

In preparing my students for oral literature fieldwork, my keen interest has been in planning for the activities is such a way that all possibilities are explored and the fieldworkers are equipped with various responses to anticipated or unexpected competing situations. There are three pairs of approaches that I have encountered in my research experience and which I normally discuss with my students. The list is not exhaustive and the reader is encouraged to come up with other scenarios that individual fieldwork experiences may deliver. The three scenarios I discuss below are exploratory versus intensive fieldwork, supervised versus independent fieldwork, and home-based versus outward bound fieldwork. Even though the categories may appear to be distinct and oppositional, in practical sense, the borderline is quite thin and the relationship more complementary. I discuss these approaches in terms of the advantages and the challenges a fieldworker is likely to encounter in employing each of them.

Exploratory Fieldwork

Oral literature fieldworkers are by nature explorers. They venture out to discover various oral art forms that exist in a given society. For instance, a fieldworker may visit Coastal region in Kenya to record oral literature of the Mijikenda. This requires covering a wide geographical area, at times within a very short time. A fieldworker operating under this approach is interested in covering, where possible, the entire community, recording all genres of oral literature existing in the community within a given period of time. The approach is quite exciting and informative to young fieldworkers who happen to be first time visitors to the research site. It is a good eye opener as it exposes one to various performances in a community, which in turn offers a rich variety of texts for comparative analysis. However the approach, if implemented solely poses formidable challenges that one should be aware of.

These challenges are logistical, economical, and analytical. My observation is that exploratory fieldworkers are hard pressed for time and therefore operate with urgency to complete the assignment. They are also more interested in the quantity of the texts collected which compromises quality. This kind of fieldwork is expensive in time, finances and skills required without any assurance on the quality of texts collected. A fieldworker may end up collecting hundreds of recordings in audio/video tapes, notes, and photographs that they may not have the capacity, time and wherewithal to analyse. This partly explains why a visit to some of the research offices in universities reveal collected texts gathering dust before analysis because collection did not take into consideration the capacity to analyse the texts. Analysis may also take too long to complete which delays the release of the research findings. In some unfortunate cases, fieldworkers die before they analyse the data and all the knowledge painstakingly generated is left to go to waste by family members who may not be aware of their research value.

In Chapter One we gave the case of Owuor Anyumba as a good local example.

Intensive Fieldwork

Intensive Fieldwork is the opposite of the exploratory approach. It focuses on the collection of specific oral texts in a particular location. For example, a fieldworker may set out to collect Maragoli wedding songs in Chavakali Ward of Vihiga County in Kenya. The exercise is concentrated on a specific genre in a specific research site which allows the fieldworker to manage the activities with minimal support. This approach is economical if well planned as it takes a short duration and ensures that only relevant material addressing the research question is collected. It also takes a short time to process the data to produce the research findings. In my research classes, I experiment a lot with this approach because it is very focused and economical in time, money, and capacity. The guiding principle in using this fieldwork approach is "less is sometimes more" (Finnegan 1992, 65). As Finnegan suggests it is profitable to cut your coat according to your size. You should decide in good time the form of documentation most appropriate to your needs and skills, limit yourself to that, and do it well instead of returning to your workstation with a heavy luggage full of inadequate field notes, insufficient recordings, and laughable photographs. One should be humbled by the harsh reality that however efficient, no fieldworker gets the ultimate quest, hence the wisdom of going for the best.

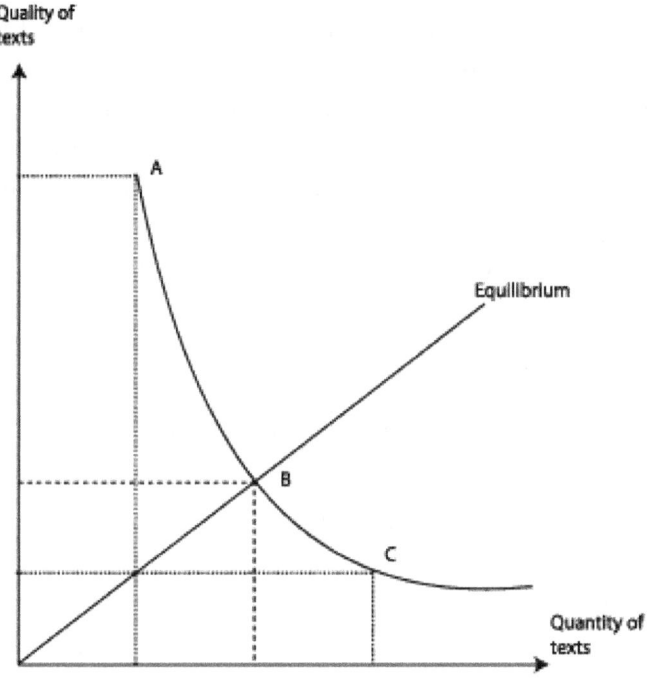

Figure 2: Diagram illustrating the relationship between quantity and quality in fieldwork

As the diagram above illustrates, there is a complementary relationship between the horizontal and longitudinal approaches to oral literature fieldwork. While the former is quantitative, the latter is qualitative. The diagram illustrates that a good oral literature fieldwork should balance interest in the number of texts and the quality that texts have. It implies that a point of equilibrium must be identified in the fieldwork design so that the optimum number of interviews and other performances are recorded within a given research period using adequate resources. The diagram also indicates that too much emphasis on quantity may render hundreds if not thousands of recorded oral texts which may be thin on quality. Conversely, keenness on quality alone may deliver a handful of excellent transcripts that cannot be subjected to detailed comparative analysis. A good fieldworker should plan to operate at point "B", which is the point of equilibrium in the diagram. It is the point at which both quantity and quality are optimal. Points "A" and "C" are extremes that should be avoided as they take researchers off balance. While exploratory research pushes one to point "C", intensive research pulls a researcher to point "A." A well designed methodology achieves a compromise at point "B".

Supervised Fieldwork

The second scenario that a researcher may encounter is supervised fieldwork as opposed to independent fieldwork. Supervised fieldwork is the research activity in which the lead researcher who may be a university lecturer, plans for fieldwork through lectures within the university, and thereafter, accompanies the research assistants or students to the field for data collection. The Department of Literature at the University of Nairobi employs this approach a lot in training residential undergraduate and postgraduate students specialising in African oral literature. The advantages of supervised fieldwork include back-stopping which ensures that should unforeseen challenges occur in the field, research assistants have an experienced team leader to rely on. This is common since young researchers normally overlook some steps critical in data collection like getting informed consent before recording voices of respondents or taking photographs that may elicit sharp reaction from some irritable community members acutely aware of either research ethics or intellectual property rights or both.

Presence of a lead researcher in the field gives the activity an official cover and insurance against failure. Community members quite often suffer from research fatigue. Their normal reaction is to doubt data collectors, especially when they are young, inexperienced and elitist. Having a senior researcher gives community members an assurance that the activity is official and geared towards the future good of the society. The lead researcher also takes off the burden of managing fieldwork logistics from the students such as organising field transport, food, accommodation, communication with local administration and identification of local research assistants. This gives students enough time to concentrate on refining methodology of data collection.

In fieldwork, we normally plan for the best but leave room for the unexpected. Cases of illnesses, deaths, arrests by law enforcement agents, or civil strife that may endanger the study and lives of researchers occur when they are least expected. Supervised fieldwork ensures that a senior researcher is available to take prompt and appropriate action to protect lives of researchers, objectives of the study, image of the university or sponsoring institution, and interests of community members. The lead researcher ensures that fieldworkers protect the integrity of the sponsoring organisation and host community by observing research ethics at all times. There is a tendency among young researchers to indulge in leisure, especially taking local brews immediately they get to the field under the guise of rapport creation. The presence of a senior researcher restraints such wayward individuals and compels them to concentrate on achieving the objectives of fieldwork before merriment. In addition, supervised research utilizes team expedition which ensures that large amounts of data are collected simultaneously in a given research expedition.

These advantages of supervised fieldwork can only be realized if the lead researcher is qualified, committed, and enthusiastic about fieldwork. I have met good researchers who are more comfortable working from their offices in the universities rather than venture into the field. Such scholars cannot guide young researchers in fieldwork even if they are professors because fieldwork only respects grounding in methodology and not academic titles. In deed, some professors who were veteran fieldworkers decades ago become a liability in modern fieldwork, especially when they have ceased active engagement but still insist on dictating how fieldwork should be undertaken oblivious of changes that have taken place in fieldwork theory, methodology and technology used. I have also observed a few disturbing cases where lead researchers behave like irresponsible tour guides. They take students to the remote research locations and leave them on their own as they engage in merriment in posh hotels or entertainment joints nearby.

Of late, the habit of some lead researchers taking students to the field and sneaking back at night to the comfort of their homes for a good sleep and returning to the field in the morning has emerged courtesy of improved road and air transport system and availability of cellular telephone services. Such conduct is unprofessional. Evenings with research assistants in the field are valuable opportunities for bonding and reviewing the day's progress in terms of the gains and the challenges. Together, the team revises the strategy to be employed the following day to build up on the gains while mitigating the setbacks suffered. Each new day in the field is supposed to be a new experience powered by the lessons learnt from the previous engagements. Staying together consistently in the field makes the learning curve move upwards at the 45^0 angle. Lead researchers have heavy responsibilities as researchers, parents, community members and ambassadors of the sponsoring research institutions. They must fulfil their mandate with honesty, diligence and decisiveness.

Our discussion of the advantages of the supervised fieldwork can easily persuade a young researcher to celebrate. It may also appear as the best approach for lead researchers as they stay in charge of the fieldwork process from its design stages at the university to data collection phase in the field and finally the data analysis phase back at the work station. Nevertheless, the approach has some challenges that one needs to be aware of to tone down premature excitement. Constant presence of a lead researcher next to young researchers can be intimidating. It denies them flexibility to devise other creative approaches in dealing with unique situations as they fear deviating from the methodology favoured by the lead researcher. Unless the fieldwork is over a longer period of time, the team may miss "a deeper understanding gained through intensive personal participation" (Finnegan 1992, 54). The approach can also encourage laziness in young researchers as they consider the study to belong to the lead researcher who will not allow it to fail, anyway. The approach is normally rigid because you have to handle the interests of all the team members; as such, minority members of the team like expectant ladies, mature students, and persons with disabilities are likely to suffer. In addition, the approach cannot work where one is training a large class. I once listened to a fellow fieldworker share his experience in one of our national universities where they had just conducted supervised fieldwork for over three hundred students. They had to use several buses and get several lecturers to assist. Majority of the lecturers co-opted into the trip had not conducted fieldwork before. He reported that the project was not successful. It was like a locust invasion. The large number of students caused environmental degradation in the hitherto quiet and clean village. They also intimidated villagers who felt invaded by rowdy youth.

Independent Fieldwork

The disadvantages of supervised fieldwork have challenged oral literature fieldworkers to find an alternative in independent fieldwork. This is a field study in which a researcher and assistants design a fieldwork project within the classroom or office environment and then physically part ways to the field. The lead researcher either remains at the research institution or proceeds to the field in his or her own capacity as a researcher and not a supervisor. The research assistants are left on their own to apply the skills learnt in class or through apprenticeship in data collection. At the University of Nairobi, I have used this approach with senior students enrolled in distance learning programme. These are mostly trained teachers or mature adults working in the countryside but are enrolled in the Bachelor of Education (Arts) degree programme offered by the university. Their number is large and they are also scattered all over the country. The nature of their programme (learning at a distance), age, family responsibilities, and work schedule make it impossible to bring them together for a supervised fieldwork.

The advantages of this approach are varied: It brings with it personal immersion in the field, a researcher feels a sense of completeness and absorption in the fieldwork which is lacking in team-based supervised fieldwork. It is flexible and therefore suitable for mature students as they have freedom to choose when to conduct fieldwork, what to research on, research location, duration of the field study and who to include in the sample. Further more, the approach is empowering as it compels fieldworkers to be creative, committed, and diligent to succeed. Fieldworkers who employ this approach and succeed emerge more mature because they not only deal with practical aspects of methodological considerations in the field, but also logistical and ethical issues, which in other scenarios are handled by a lead researcher. Failure, for majority of adult learners, is never an option especially in fieldwork. In normal circumstances young fieldworkers yearn for independence to prove their worth as researchers and solitary approach proffers them this opportunity. Independent research is cost effective since fieldworkers operate in environments they are familiar with, which makes their fieldwork cheap and enjoyable. The logic is that it is easier to manage the expenses of an individual than a group. This is because an individual researcher can use local cost cutting measures like local transport, spending nights with relatives or at home and speeding up data collection to reduce days spent in the field.

In employing an independent approach to fieldwork, one should be aware of the challenges one is likely to encounter either as a lead researcher or a data collector. They include time wastage due to procrastination, distraction, spiralling cost in community contributions, temptation to plagiarise works of other researchers, and lack of capacity to deal with unexpected field challenges. When a data collector is alone in the field, it requires high level of discipline to keep to the schedules. There is always a tendency to want to do it later. Laxity leads to procrastination which robs even a good fieldworker of quality time to collect valuable data. One can assess how time-conscious the fieldworker is by comparing the quantity and quality of the recordings done against the days and money spent in the field. There should be a balance. An independent researcher has a lot of freedom that can be abused, especially when the researcher decides to be distracted from the core activity by other unrelated competing activities in the research location like ceremonies.

One of the major assumptions of this approach is that the fieldworker is mature, honest and committed to the ideals of sound scholarship. Experience has, however, taught me that a number of mature students joining continuing education programme are driven more by the desire to get certificates to facilitate their promotion in workplaces rather than acquisition of knowledge. Such students never spare time for fieldwork and frequently fall into the temptation of plagiarism. More so, these researchers, though mature in age and life-experiences are young in terms of methodological grounding. They therefore lack the capacity to deal with unexpected field challenges. My assessment of this approach is that lack of supervision may sound appealing, but it usually leads to a poor learning experience where students are intellectually weak.

Home-based Fieldwork

The third and the last research scenario I have encountered is the home-based versus outward bound research. Desire to record performances in a culturally familiar environment is always strong in fieldworkers. Researchers operating within this approach often prefer retreating to their home areas or places where they are familiar for data collection, hence the term home-based research. It is the most logical thing to do if a research opportunity presents itself. This approach has a number of advantages to a fieldworker which include ease in data collection due to prior knowledge of the local terrain and oral artists. The fieldworker is conversant with the community and the local language which reduces fear of the unknown. One is also able to conceal the identity of a researcher and collect a lot of information using participant observation method.

Generally, the researcher enjoys the company of friends and relatives who offer their services as volunteers thus eliminating the need for paid-up assistants. Costs of food, travel and tokens are incredibly low because the fieldworker is considered as 'our own daughter or son'. Messerschmidt notes that an advantage for conducting fieldwork in a culturally familiar environment is that a researcher does not have to 'go native' in the research setting because he/she is already a 'native' (8). Fieldworkers 'go native' if they try in every conceivable fashion to adopt the way of life of the common people being studied like living in their residences, eating their food, talking their language, and sharing their lives. Such conduct is often difficult to sustain, because the researcher is attempting to learn the role of a local and responsible adult while also conducting research and maintaining field notes and a field diary (Cassell, 33). Prior knowledge of the fieldwork locale gives fieldworkers added advantage which makes data collection easier compared to if they were foreign investigators (Nukunya, 19).

Home-based approach, like the others we have discussed before, has some challenges that one needs to be aware of. Familiarity, as the old saying goes, "breeds contempt and can jeopardize research work" (Aguilar, 24). Researchers may assume that they will receive automatic acceptance in their places of birth in terms of work or residence only to wake up to a rude shock about the deep-rooted dislike for them, sometimes based on long standing feuds between families or clans. These 'own-culture-studies,' as Finegann (1992) terms this approach, bring not only an insider's understanding but also problems, especially the difficulty of seeing the findings from a comparative and detached viewpoint and of being aware of the perhaps privileged or interested nature of one's own experience (55). Furthermore, home-based research demands that a fieldworker pretends to be a stranger in his own village by feigning ignorance of common knowledge about the research topic, which community members, mostly friends, relatives and colleagues are sure the researcher knows too well.

This introduces the dilemma of convincing people to give you information that you know they know you already have. When you operate in a familiar setting, it becomes challenging to get people to stop seeing you as, Kamau or Halima, their friend or family and to treat you as Kamau or Halima, the researcher. Depending on your lifestyle, they may even think that fieldwork is just one of the many jokes you habitually play on them during your visits.

The approach is uneconomical in time management because by going to the village or community of one's residence, the researcher submits to the authority of decision makers in the community. The researcher must therefore participate in community activities like funerals, weddings, land tribunals and other local and at times partisan activities as prioritised by the elders. The high risk that this approach exposes a fieldworker to is partisanship. A fieldworker is a human being with feelings, biases, and the history of the community. They are committed to some values, beliefs and principles. The more committed a fieldworker is to a particular faction in the locality, the less one can learn, at first hand, about others.

The study may suffer from clan feuds which may constrain sampling of good artists and interviewees. For instance, if the researcher or a close member of the family has been having a court case with a good artist in the same community, it may be impossible for the researcher to approach this artist for a performance. Another problem in taking on a partisan role as a researcher is that it almost inevitably causes bias in favour of those to whom one is committed. Due to human nature, it may be irresistible taking sides in the field. Obviously, researchers will identify with respondents who make their work easier. It is nevertheless advisable that the researcher remains focused on achieving research objectives by "maintaining close informants on opposing sides, and try, in the analysis of events, to be on guard against personal biases" (Komblum, 241).

I have had opportunity to guide some of my students during fieldwork in their home areas. On such occasions, I have discovered that if one is not careful in managing goodwill and material generosity in their home areas during fieldwork, they may end up impoverishing host community members. The generosity of the hosts, to one of their own, can be incredibly amazing. They not only volunteer their time but also prepare food for the researcher, some times at a great personal sacrifice. This in turn demands that researchers reciprocate accordingly. The cost of fieldwork can therefore end up being higher in one's home area because one feels compelled to reciprocate appropriately.

I had opportunity to visit a colleague I was supervising on fieldwork for a doctoral dissertation in July 2008. He was among his kith and kin and the level of generosity from one host-artist was unbelievable. Although we arrived at the home of the artist, who is a respected elder in the mid morning, he insisted that we wait for breakfast to be served before he could perform. I looked with sympathy as his wife, equally advanced in age, struggled to prepare a good breakfast for the 'guests'. Once tea and slices of bread were served, he instructed the wife to start preparing chicken for lunch immediately. The preparation of lunch involved chasing the cock that was roaming in the compound oblivious of the conspiracy. The old lady was supposed to mobilise young people in the neighbourhood to help her in catching the cock. I looked at my student-researcher hopping he would decline politely, but he was more keen on collecting data than discussing food matters. When I noticed he was not going to intervene, I interjected by thanking the artist for the offer of lunch. I explained politely that because we had other interviews lined up in other locations (which was not true), we would only record the performances and visit again later to stay longer with the family. Immediately we left the generous artist, I softly reprimanded the researcher that one does not have to accept all offers from hosts to appear respectful. He exonerated himself politely arguing that in this particular community stopping your host from giving you a treat of a good meal is culturally reprehensible, especially if it is chicken which is a local delicacy. We laughed away the incident with a reminder to him that a home-based fieldworker needs to know the thin line between promoting congeniality and profligacy.

Picture of the generous artist (left)in Bungoma North District interviewed by Kimingichi Wabende *Picture by Peter Wasamba July 2008*

Outward-bound Fieldwork

As opposed to home-based fieldwork, a number of fieldworkers are driven by the desire to learn more about communities they have never come into contact with. This dare-devil approach entails visiting and collecting data in an unfamiliar environment where a researcher has no prior association and (or) language competence. For example, a researcher from the Coast Province of Kenya who chooses to collect data in Northern Kenya, where they have never been residents before, would be employing the outward-bound approach. I experienced the extreme case when I embarked on fieldwork in Seoul Metropolitan Region (SMR) in South Korea between 2010 and 2012. The place, people, weather, food, belief systems, language and alphabets were completely alien to me. The advantages of this approach include impartiality by the researcher which increases objectivity in research. The fieldworker remains focused on the purpose of the visit and is not easily distracted by irrelevant community engagements. The approach promotes creativity, cultural understanding and tolerance as the researcher is able to empathetically identify with the host community. Further, the approach empowers the researchers as they are compelled by circumstances to overcome several challenges as visitors and researchers. Outsiders in many cases enjoy privileges of visitors. They are perceived as sympathetic foreign researchers with the interest of the community at heart. This earns a 'stranger-value' to a fieldworker as reflected in the level of hospitality and openness from local informants.

A Pokot warrior being interviewed in Sigor, West Pokot June 2005, an example of outward bound fieldwork, *Picture by Peter Wasamba*

The disadvantages of this approach include language problem which necessitates over-reliance on local assistants. The researcher does not have "the insider's familiarity with local perceptions, experience and language" (Finnegan 1992, 55). One cannot avoid the challenges of translation which depends, to a large extent, on the language competence of the local assistant. It is normally assumed, erroneously though, that a research assistant is equally competent in the language of the community and that of the research. In many cases, they are only competent in one language which creates communication lacuna.

Operating in a new environment, removed from one's learning environment introduces a security angle to fieldwork, even if the area is classified by government officials as safe. There is a sense in which being a stranger acts as a magnet to petty criminals in the locality who get encouraged by the supposition that researchers have valuables like money or expensive items and that they are not likely to fight back aggressively when attacked. It should not be forgotten that we operate in the era of terrorism. Fieldworkers can be attacked, kidnapped or denied access to information based on the perceived unfriendly policy of a country or ethnic community they belong to. Outward bound research is generally expensive due to the high cost of local assistants who demand excessive payments, due to the misplaced notion that fieldwork activities are generously funded. A word of caution: whereas many fieldworkers venture into unknown communities fearful and planning to complete the field research within the shortest period possible, the host communities tend to be warm and caring which in turn confounds fieldworkers. Perplexed by the unexpected, some fieldworkers forget the ethical distance and melt completely into the community, which may delay the completion of the study.

Our discussion of the various approaches to fieldwork has indicated that each approach has its strengths and challenges. There is no need, therefore, to look down on any approach or to romanticise one approach as the finest. The best combination brings together strengths of various approaches to address the research question based on the total circumstances surrounding the study.

Theory and Oral Literature

This chapter debates the place of theory in oral literature scholarship. There is already rich literature on theories, ranging from ancient to contemporary, applicable to oral literature. What, in my assessment, is lacking among young scholars of oral literature is the mental disposition to theorize with positive attitude. In this chapter I expose the workings of a theoretical mind, without taking particular positions on specific theories, and leave the reader to choose the appropriate tool to use. In the previous chapters, I demonstrated that oral literature is multi-disciplinary in origin, nature and functions. Linguists, ethnologists, sociologists, and anthropologists, for example, were among the earliest scholars to notice the value of the spoken word in their disciplines. These disciplines have continued to make significant contributions to oral literature scholarship, research, and theoretical growth. In deed, if theories that oral literature borrows from linguistics and anthropology are taken away, the discipline would remain theoretically half-naked since the genre cannot be serviced adequately by literary theories alone. It is therefore quite challenging to fence off oral literature from the neighbouring disciplines in social sciences and humanities without stifling its development. It is even more intricate to situate oral literature exclusively in humanities or social sciences due to its "border-operator" characteristics. The theoretical "in-betweenness" of oral literature is exacerbated by the rigidity of the existing literary theories formulated with the written text in mind. This leaves oral literature no option but to be an adoptive child of a disciplinary universe that employs ethnographic theories and methodologies while maintaining fidelity to its literary habitat. Oral literature cannot, for that reason, have a theory that is exclusively its own as it is intertwined with other disciplines that have made contributions to its growth.

The place of theory in oral literature scholarship has engaged the thinking of scholars within and outside the discipline for years. Questions that have dominated the debate include: What is African oral literature? What is the canon in African oral literature? What is the place of theory in African oral literature scholarship? Which are the dominant theories of oral literature? Must fieldwork be conducted within a defined theoretical framework? Should oral literature scholars use theories borrowed from social sciences and linguistics? Who are the African theoreticians? Is theory dead? And, why bother? Scholars like Stanley Fish, concede that "Theory's day is dying: the hour is late, and the only thing left for a theorist to do is to say so" (341). Other scholars are over optimistic and are prematurely celebrating the expansion of theory to new frontiers. Bauman, for instance, observes that folklore scholarship has conquered its theoretical frontiers and must now seek to establish "settlements" (Limon and Young, 438-9).

My undergraduate students often displayed mixed reactions when theory was introduced as an academic course unit. One category thought that theory limits academic freedom, aggravates mental torture, and that apart from it being a requirement for students to pass their exams, it was meant to achieve very little in terms of awakening logical sensibilities, analytical instincts and precise application of concepts. Another group of students, normally small in number but adventurous in spirit, expressed excitement at the possibility of learning new tools of analysis, conquering new horizons of intellectual landscape, and acquiring new vocabulary for explaining meanings deduced from their inquisitions.

Then there was the last category you will meet in an average undergraduate class; the bandwagon. This category had no position at all and easily supported the most vocal group, often the first category. The only difference was that they were not able to explain their decision to treat theory with detachment and cynicism. The three positions towards theory explained above may tempt one to wonder whether scholarship was created for theory or theory for scholarship. Lethargy to theory is a reflection of weaknesses in its pedagogy. Theory has frequently been misrepresented in academic discourse, misunderstood, misused, and condemned out of ignorance or prejudice. Scholars have been scared by the purported technicality of theory and its mutative existence.

Theory and Scholarship

Theory is not meant to be a gate-keeper to knowledge generation; the relationship between theory and scholarship is symbiotic. Theory is nourished by a vibrant intellectual climate that gives it life and expands its horizon. Intellectuals too need theory as a compass to get their bearing in the vast jungle of knowledge. Theory, hence, is neither an epistemological roadblock through which all knowledge is screened, purified, and sanctified nor is it a philosophical disputation without end. I consider theories as sages who are quiet but thoughtful, reflective and perceptive. They sympathetically observe how young thinkers are engaged in tacit struggles to understand the what? how? and why? of the phenomena. Without intruding, they let the young ones go on with their quests.

The inquisitors, who want to see common things differently, recognise the sages' presence, wealth of wisdom, and depth of perception and pay homage to them for intellectual armament and inspiration. They borrow from the philosophers wisdom, cogitation and specific lenses to perceive concepts clearly and state their claims convincingly. These lenses and accompanying accessories are given on condition that the wearers convert to passionate advocates who only see, evaluate, and explain what is captured through the new 'eyes' and mental disposition. In this way, theory is not imposed on users. Scholars willingly choose to apply theory to their work to see old things anew or the reverse. They pick on theory(ies) that can work best for them based on their ability to see what they want to see and how they want to see it. They are also free to drop theories, modify them, or complement them with others if they are inadequate on their own.

Based on the argument advanced, does it therefore imply that engagement with theory is optional in scholarship? Could it be that I am suggesting theory can successfully be avoided altogether? Can a grand inquirer face the jungle of knowledge intellectually bare-handed without tools of perception, analysis, and interpretation? Can knowledge be grasped *ex-nihilo*? Catherine Besley in *Critical Practice* (1980) warns that "There is no practice without theory, however much that theory is suppressed, unformulated or perceived as 'obvious'" (4). Ron Grele, a North American oral historian, similarly lamented in 1975 about the limited critical discussion among oral historians about the theoretical and methodological issues underpinning their work (Perks and Thomson, xi). Besley's and Grele's positions are reinforced by Masheti Masinjila who adds that, regardless of what one may refer to as a theory of oral literature, consciously or unconsciously, scholars operate within a "coherent set of conceptual, hypothetical and pragmatic principles which form the general frame of reference for a discipline" (1).

The very nature of oral literature as a discourse makes it allergic to a theoretical vacuum. Oral literature exists in four forms: the original oral interview or performance, the recorded version of the interview, the written transcript and the interpretation of the interview material. The performance itself is not just a means to an end; it is a communicative event. And, as such, it needs to be given theoretical reflection (Abrams, 10). Oral literature, as a discipline, cannot thus be studied outside theory. There is need to bolster the theoretical basis of the discipline by recognizing the historical and social dimensions of folklore as communicative action (Muana, 2).

Theory is from the Greek word *theoria* which refers to passionate, neutral, and sympathetic contemplation of knowledge. It precedes *gnosis*, which refers to "practice." The word "theory" means a number of different things, depending on the context. In natural sciences, any hypothesis that on invention explains various large and independent classes of facts ascends to the coveted pedestal of theory. In humanities, "theory" refers to the non-practical aspect of the intellectual engagement which includes unproven ideas and speculation. If we chain the three Greek words *theorea, gnosis,* and *praxis* (work or action), we get to locate the continuum of theory from contemplation to awareness or knowledge generation which, ultimately leads to action in terms of practical application.

Theory is not monolithic. It is highly contextual and resists confinement. Various approaches to theory are intertwined with social and political processes as well as wider intellectual movements of the time. In assessing existing or emerging theories one must go beyond the technical terms to be in sync with the prevalent "social and ethical" issues (Finnegan 1992: 28). The truth about theory vary greatly in character and coloration depending on where we choose to stand, what aspects we elect to emphasize, what period we wish to concentrate on, what art form, what aspect, what line of significance, tradition of influence, or national lineage we might like to chase and what broad deduction one cares to make (Bradbury, 765). Achebe's explanation of African Mask dancing can help in understanding Finnegan and Bradbury's arguments. Theory is analogous to an African mask dancing. If you want to understand it and enjoy it, you do not observe from one position, you keep on going round. It does not surprise me that theory is fragmented into multiple bickering intellectual siblings. The landscape, at face value, exemplifies harmony in discord. It is amazing that from this cacophony of discordant voices emerges the gem of distilled thoughts of men and women endowed with positional knowledge and experience. Interestingly enough, it is such academic and intellectual quarrels that sustain scholarship:

> There is nothing wrong with academic and intellectual quarrels;
> thought would hardly be doing a service, universities would scarcely
> exist, historians would be a dull constituency indeed, if we didn't
> constantly engage in such wars of interpretation and
> reinterpretation, definition and counter-definition. (Bradbury, 764)

As Bradbury contends, beyond this din of cognitive dissonance, there emerges a powerful dialectical wave of epistemic harmony that enables theories to gravitate towards accommodation and ontological consonance. I can equate theory creation and nurturing to coming to birth. Conception and pre-natal care are phases that demand utmost care before delivery which is the most painful time in theory formulation. Thereafter, the arduous task of keeping theory on a steady growth through childhood, acceptance, application, maturation, modification, aging, death and possible reincarnation become even more demanding. The polyphonic nature of theoretical discourse is not a disadvantage. It is theory's main strength in that "different perspectives provide different forms of knowledge about a phenomenon so that, together, they produce a broader understanding" (Jørgensen and Phillips, 4). As Bruce Lincoln fittingly elaborates, "questioning" or "perceiving at a tangent" is a mark of theorization because theoreticians:

> ... exist within a time, a place, and a social situation, and their speech, thought and interests originate in, reflect, and engage these givens of their own experience in some measure, although this is not all that they do. Still, the books and articles which scholars write and the lectures they give are not just descriptive accounts of something that unproblematically 'is'. Rather, these are synthetic constructions which partake in varying degrees of the people who are speaking, that of whom they speak, and those to whom their speech is addressed. Such processes can be extremely accurate, revealing, and enlightening; but they can never be perfectly neutral and disinterested, no matter how much those who are involved as speakers or hearers may sincerely take them to be so. (Lincoln, xvii)

Lincoln brings out the acme of theorization; it is based on individual's positionality, abnormality of thought, and an element of cynicism. Theoreticians defy strong waves of contemporary thought prevalent in their time to chart alternative ways of perception and interpretation. They are always suspicious about communication and instinctively doubt what is generally taken to be true, is plausibly true, or is talked about as true. In many cases, they discover a mismatch between "what is communicated" and "what is" about a given phenomenon. They come in to provide an alternative (fresh) way of seeing "what is" and also "how to communicate what is." They avoid the trodden paths of thought and courageously face the intellectual jungle to clear new ways to explaining phenomena. It can therefore be argued that theoreticians work contrary to the dominant contemporary thought. They are lone rangers allergic to dogmas and givens.

Theory in Oral Literature

Oral literature, due to its profoundly interdisciplinary nature is, in the words of Lynn Abrams, theoretically "promiscuous" compared to other disciplines in humanities and social sciences. It picks up the shiny, attractive theories which have originated elsewhere and applies them to its own field of study (32). Oral literature scholars with a literary background are notorious for territoriality. They have a lukewarm attitude to scholars from other disciplines who assert their authority in the interpretation of interviews and performances. It has since been deduced that the spirited defence of "textuality" was driven more by protest based on the fear of the overtly sociological direction that the discipline was taking. It was feared that it was "slouching toward ethnography" (Wilgus, 1973). It is undeniable that these "unwelcome visitors" bring with them more theoretical worth from their mother disciplines and therefore add value to the discipline. Whereas oral literature is promiscuous as a discipline, the practitioners within it are theoretical pirates. They unapologetically pick and use theories from other disciplines and modify them slightly whenever the need arises.

Theory is important in oral literature scholarship because it facilitates literary criticism. It aids the interpretation and synthesis of ideas and concepts expressed within the aesthetic mode. In different ways, theory attempts to define what may be considered a plausible explanation of the phenomena observed. As we have intimated elsewhere, it also advances scholarship in oral literature from *gnosis* to *praxis* through critical ethnography. Brown and Sidney, reflecting on the emergence of critical ethnography in the "Introduction: New Writers of the Cultural Sage," observe that as critical ethnography rediscovers its own theoretical and pedagogical legs, it is beginning to move beyond the issues of postmodern critique that gave birth to it, to immerse itself in "critical praxis: a praxis that is theoretically informed, methodologically dialectical, and politically and ethically oriented" (3). The new theory, according to the duo, in commenting on its critics, succeeds in liberating itself from the reductive, contradictory chains of postmodern signification, thereby evolving a critical praxis that is at once emergent and immersed. This reconfigured praxis seeks to actualize both aspects of the Freirean educational dialectic in which critical analysis of localized and politicized problem is but a spring board into meaningful action to mitigate, legislate, or eliminate those problems (4- 5).

As a performance based discipline, oral literature is encountered "out there" in the field. An oral literature scholar is invariably a fieldworker. Fieldwork benefits from theoretical consciousness. In order to record and process performances that can be analyzed and used by all the research participants, fieldwork must be based on theory. It should be clarified that theoretical focalization does not in any way imply imposing ideas into an already preconceived framework. In addition, it does not entail imposing a theory on a study for mere academic correctness; theoretical grounding means that scholarship follows a roadmap of explainable processes or procedures that a researcher may or may not be conscious of at the time of the study.

Theoretical consciousness is critical to successful fieldwork since "all the major steps like review of relevant literature, sampling, transcribing, analysis and interpretation constitute theorising" (Weaver and Atkinson, 20). Theory, further, determines what counts as relevant data in the exploration of a given research problem and determines what may be regarded as a respectable research agenda in a given field. I must emphasize that scholars do not have to declaim extravagantly the theory or theories they purport to use. In many cases a keen reader discovers a wide gap between the theory pompously stated in a document and the data analysis that follows. Frequently, students writing research papers or theses assemble a bundle of theories they intend to use without really intending to use any. Whereas such papers have high sounding theories in their theoretical frameworks, the data presentation that follows is pedestrian and devoid of structured perspectival thinking. Gaps between theories stated and analyses generated indicate inadequate training in critical thinking in the formative stages of scholarship.

Critical thinking cannot be taught as a stand-alone course. It has to be demonstrated in the delivery of the content in all the disciplines. Critical thinking, which is amenable to theorization, is reflected in the cogency of the arguments, relentless questioning, penetrating insights, queer thinking, and the academic architecture of scholars. Majority of students are exposed to theories without understanding what critical thinking and conceptualization mean. Theory is then reduced to a camouflage for researchers without any clear orientation. In some cases, scholars take to theory with the passion of a religious crusader. They end up suffering from constipation caused by an overdose of theoretically indigestible combinations.

My suggestion is that theory should be operationalized and not dramatized. It should be allowed to demonstrate its robustness in the choice, arrangement, and the subsequent interpretation of data. Soyinka's famous argument in dismissing negritudists who were nostalgic about the lost Africa's primal beauty may clarify the argument. Soyinka argued that a tiger does not shout its tigritude, it pounces. In the same way, a theory does not have to be named; its' architecture in data handling should define it to the reader. In this respect, theory is given freedom to continuously engage the reader or audience in a conversation without a biased intrusion by the researcher or writer. It becomes a healthy dialogue between two trusting parties; the reader and the theory.

Oral literature is dialogic and discursive and therefore invites employment of theories to interpret the significance of performances to the narrator. Key to this approach is the acknowledgement that the performance or interview is "a conversational narrative" or a "communicative event" that has taken place in real time between real people (Joyner in Abrams, 16). Wanjiku Kabira captures the conversational nature of a performance thus:

> A good narrator uses his skill to develop and embroider the skeleton of the available plot with subsidiary details. His own vivid descriptions and songs, his actual style of delivery, gestures,

mimicry and use of dramatic repetition are also skilfully interwoven. The way he presents his characters, his variation of speed and tone, vocabulary, persuasion of his listeners, vehemence and drama, are all knit into an aesthetic whole (Kabira 1983, 16).

Commenting on the *udje* poetry among the Urhobo of Nigeria, Godini Darah, like Wanjiku Kabira observes that the performance of *udje* poetry is a serious communicative event in which the artist is pushed to the limit of creativity and performance:

The language, idiom, and imagery are dense and wide-ranging. The realms of ideas, thoughts, and fields of knowledge explored in the songs are deep and comprehensive; the emotions and feelings are lofty and sublime and the melodic and tonal variations are musical and memorable. The performance of the dance theatre is spectacular and the costumes and accoutrement of the artists are gorgeous and ostentatious. Whenever udje is performed, the average Urhobo person feels spiritually fulfilled and aesthetically renewed. (4)

Such rich performances cannot be handled in a theoretical void. Fieldwork therefore offers young researchers opportunity to discuss theories of oral literature in class and test them in the field. Through fieldwork in oral literature, students learn that no theory is cast on stone and students have to be alert at all times to the theoretical frameworks they employ in their study with a view to customising them to fit within their specific situations. In situations where students have not picked any specific thinking to follow, they should be alert to document the processes and procedures followed in research because these constitute theorizing. In designing fieldwork projects, researchers grapple with questions that respond to feminist, postcolonial, and poststructuralist theoretical perspectives on experience and knowledge and which highlight the partiality and historicity of knowledge and experience of both the "informant's" and also the researcher's (Horner, 14).

Traditional Theories of Oral Literature

Looking back at the theoretical landscape of the 19th and early 20th Centuries, one notes that many theories of this era were grounded in cultural studies. They were concerned with the history of particular forms of verbal art in terms of origins, diffusion, evolution, or functions. To get to grips with all the different elements that surface in an oral literature encounter in the contemporary society, scholars have had to exploit theories such as cultural evolutionism, diffusionism, structuralism, post-structuralism, post-modernism, deconstruction, reader response, feminist criticism, queer theory, grounded theory, new historicism and many others. As I mentioned at the beginning of this chapter, there is already an over-supply of literature regarding all these theories. An exploratory discussion of some of the theories undertaken here does not in any way replace individual engagement with the theories. At best, it retains the spirit of theoretical pluralism, multi-disciplinary engagement and continuous dialogue about oral literature and contemplation. I remain focused in my goal to demystify theory, revive debate in theory, and encourage oral literature students to invest in theoretical re-engineering.

Plato and Aristotle remain the earliest scholars to open up debate on the nature and role of art in society. In *The Republic*, Plato is remembered for his attack on poetry, along with other forms of what he called *mimesis*. He argued that most of it should be banned from the ideal society that he described in *The Republic*. According to Plato, art is removed from any notion of real truth, an inherently flawed copy of an already imperfect world; as an imitation art is irrelevant to what is real. He differentiates literary genres on the basis of the genre-specific constellation of two fundamental modes of speech termed *mimesis*, the direct imitation of speech in the form of the characters' verbatim dialogues and monologues, and *diegesis*, which comprises all utterances that can be attributed to the author.

Mimesis does not tell; it shows by means of directly-represented action that is enacted. *Diegesis*, however, is the telling of the story by a narrator; the author narrates action indirectly and describes what is in the characters' minds and emotions. The narrator may speak as a particular character or may be the invisible narrator or even the all-knowing narrator who speaks from above in the form of commenting on the action or the characters. According to Plato, the lyric genre is restricted to the use of *diegesis* and the dramatic genre to the use of *mimesis*, with only the epic genre combining both. This fundamental distinction of the two principal modes of narrating anticipated the 20th-century opposition *showing* vs. *telling* (Meister, 23). Plato favours *diegesis* to mimesis and he wrote *The Republic* in dramatic dialogue based on the principle of *digesis*.

Aristotle, Plato's former student, is equally concerned with the value of art in society and the impact that a poet is likely to have on others. He differs with Plato in his interpretation of *mimesis*. The two, however, concur in their elucidation of *diegesis*. Aristotle was the first to introduce the theory that art imitates nature and he considered the origin of art as a basis for his argument. Aristotle attributed the origin of art to the human affinity for imitation. He concluded that it is natural for humans to delight in works of imitation. In responding to Plato's apprehension that art, especially tragedy, corrupts the mind and leads to uncalled for emotional instability, Aristotle introduced the concept of catharsis. Aristotle argues that a work of art may arouse feelings of pity and fear, but it also cures these feelings through catharsis.

Aristotle's *Poetics* presents a second criterion that is fundamental for the understanding of narrative: the distinction between the totality of events taking place in a depicted world and the *muthos* (the narrated plot or storyline of a play). He points out that the latter is always a construct presenting a subset of events, chosen and arranged according to aesthetic considerations. This resulted in the *Poetics'* functional approach to fictional protagonists and their actions, the latter explained as governed by the aesthetic and logical requirements of the overall *muthos* (Meister, 56). Plato and Aristotle, in their quest to locate the nature and functions of art, become the pioneer theoreticians in the study of narrative.

Ethnology, the branch of cultural Anthropology that studies human cultures in terms of: social structure, language, religion, and technology contributed to the study of oral literature through cultural evolutionism and cultural diffusionism. Cultural evolution as a theory in anthropology developed in the 19th century as an outgrowth of the Darwinian Theory of Evolution. Evolutionism was premised on the understanding that all human societies emerged from a single society before progressing through a series of uniform stages from primitive to more advanced ones. The theory was based on the understanding that all human societies evolve along a common track from simple hunting and gathering communities to literate civilizations. All societies must pass through the same standard sequence of stages in vertical progression. They observed that the only variable in this case was the speed of movement from one stage to another. Some societies would move faster, while laggards would totter behind. This school was guided by the belief in one way progress, parallel development, and interest in origin of cultural traits. The weaknesses of this approach included too much generalization; polarized view of society in terms of "us" versus "them," ignorance of the artistic merit in the texts and lack of contemporary relevance.

Cultural Diffusionism is a response to some of the weaknesses inherent in the cultural evolutionism. The diffusionism school was not fundamentally opposed to the evolutionists. It was only opposed to the interpretation of cultural development offered by evolutionists. They argued that similarities in cultural traits are caused by contacts and borrowings. They devoted their effort to documenting and analyzing oral texts to identify their origin, history, and geography. Specifically, they looked for the origin of a text, cause of dissemination, the route followed, and versions of the texts. Cultural diffusionism theory was propagated by a group of Austro-German anthropologists, led by Fritz Graebner, Wilhelm Schmidt, and William Graham Sumner who rejected 19th-century evolutionism in favour of a belief that a few core cultures influenced all later societies. This diffusion or spreading of culture traits from one source to other destinations was believed to be the basic force in human development.

Of the three theoreticians, Fritz Robert Graebner (1877 – 1934), a German ethnologist, stands out. He is best known for developing the theory of culture circle which became popular in the early twentieth century. Graebner did not accept the unilinear model of cultural evolution propagated by evolutionism; instead, he proposed a limited number of culture circles from which all other cultures developed through the acquisition of various cultural elements. He regarded cultural diffusion, or transfer based on some form of contact between societies, as the mechanism by which cultural traits spread. He thought that similarities between cultures were the result of cultural influences based on contacts and borrowings, rather than on a universal human nature.

There are four main types of cultural diffusion: expansion diffusion; relocation diffusion; hierarchical diffusion; and contagious diffusion. Expansion diffusion takes place when an innovation or idea that has developed in a source area expands to other areas while remaining strong at its source. Relocation diffusion happens when an idea or innovation migrates *in toto* to new areas, leaving no trace or link to its source. Hierarchical diffusion takes place when an idea or innovation cascades downwards from its source in a larger place to smaller places. Contagious diffusion is driven by person-to-person contact within a given population. Through this kind of fellowship, an idea or innovation moves from one culture to another. There are three categories of diffusion mechanisms: direct, forced, and indirect influence. Direct diffusion occurs when two cultures operate so close to each other, that it results in intermarriage and trade. Forced diffusion occurs when one culture conquers another culture and forces its own customs on the subdued people, like what colonialism did in Africa and other parts of the world. Indirect diffusion happens when traits are passed from one culture through a middleman to another culture, without the initial and subsequent cultures ever being in direct contact.

The concept of diffusion, compared to evolutionism, is easy to understand and relate to. However, like other theories, consistency in application of diffusionism is problematic. For instance, if we assume that some African cultural traits have been found in Sumatra, Indonesia, the process of locating the original text in Africa, the path followed, the variants along the way, and the authentic text in the recipient society can be a cumbersome, expensive, and endless effort. In a society where nationalism is associated with ethnocentricism, arrogance, exclusion, and jingoism, the "mother culture" mentality can be abused for racial, ethnic, political, and economic domination. Theorisation is speculative, but speculation is not infinite. Diffusion takes speculation too far as it is almost impossible to locate the original text in a specific locale. Another criticism that has been levelled at cultural diffusion is the failure to explain why certain items are *not* diffused to the recipient cultures. For example, the Agikuyu of Kenya is a dominant linguistic and economic powerhouse. It has influenced the neighbouring communities including the Kamba, Embu, Meru, Mbeere and Maasai, and still remains ahead of these communities in terms of entrepreneurial skills. How come diffusion is partial and selective? Who decides what is diffused and what is blocked or retained by the source culture?

Budding researchers in oral literature often have to contend with the challenge of whether or not to use western based theories. I did mention earlier the disquiet that oral literature scholars have about the perceived encroachment into their territory by scholars from other disciplines. The same suspicion is extended to what is perceived as a bundle of western theories imposed on African researchers. Masheti Masinjila observes that western theories, when applied to the study of African oral literature, suffer from several limitations, especially in responding to the context of the performances and the artists' contribution to the texts. He argues that resorting to some of these *ancient theories* (italics for emphasis), while useful for comparative purposes, has a limitation owing to the fact that most of them have their basis in fieldwork carried among European communities, whose findings are subjected to their understanding of oral literature (8). While Masinjila tries to be academic in his criticism of western theories, Wole Soyinka (1978) is more direct.

Soyinka blames African scholars' over-dependence on western theories on lack of "theoretical audacity." He argues that, by willingly applying western based theories to conduct studies on

African oral literature, Africans have resubmitted to theoretical colonialism:

> We... have been blindly invited to submit ourselves to a second epoch of colonization this time by the universal humanoid abstraction defined and conducted by individuals whose theories and prescriptions are derived from the apprehension of their world and their history, their social neuroses and their value systems. It is time, clearly to respond to this new threat (x).

My concern regarding Soyinka's argument is that the language he uses impedes the very delivery and therefore receipt of the message he seeks to send to fellow African audience; he writes in difficult English that even native English speakers are challenged to understand. If language is truly a medium of communication and a courier of culture, then Soyinka has been Anglicized and is speaking to the wrong audience. Language politics aside, Soyinka's position is not entirely correct. While he acceptably identifies the problem of theoretical lethargy in Africa, his attempt to explain it on North-South historical divide is more ideological than academic. My discomfort with Soyinka's intellectual activism about theory is that it encourages scape-goating instead of facing the challenge he identifies.

I have stated that theories neither impose themselves on users nor close themselves up to customization. Most important, new theories stem from the existing dominant thoughts. Soyinka's concerns raise questions of universality and particularities in theorization. It begs explanations as to what is really important in a theory: the geographical origin of theory; its tenets; or the tools that the theory provides? How come African scholars have

not agitated for an African theory of space propulsion or an
African version of Isaac Newton's law of motion? Theories are
not fixed and nobody is compelled to use exclusively one theory.
Theories are constantly modified and customized by users to
meet the latter's intellectual needs. Moreover, theories have been
able to develop various strands to accommodate cultural,
historical, gender, and geographical peculiarities. What Soyinka
is proposing is akin to theoretical apartheid which post-colonial
theories have effectively demolished. Post-colonial theories
operate under the principle that theory is always grounded in a
cultural specificity and that theory and criticism are always
material practices that are ideologically stimulated and
historically positioned.

Modern Theories of Oral Literature

The future of oral literature research in Africa inevitably lies in
theoretical eclecticism. One of the theories that lends itself to
application in multicultural contexts is the grounded theory.
From its inception in the seminal text *The Discovery of Grounded
Theory* (Glaser and Strauss 1974) to its methodological
refinement (Strauss and Corbin 1990), grounded theory's appeal
is essentially the generation of theory from data. It foregrounds
textual, visual, or sound data as the source of theory. The
constant comparative method integral to grounded theory is
presented as a manual step-by-step qualitative data analysis:
inductive category coding based on "units of meaning" of textual
data, refinement of categories, exploration of relationship, and
patterns across categories leading up to an integration of data or

sense-making (Maykut and Morehouse, 126). Grounded theory encourages the use of coding in analysing texts.

Though it is employed by social scientists, the approach has not found a comfortable home in oral literature research, especially among literary scholars who cringe at any idea that suggests, even remotely, a statistical engagement. The matter has not been helped by social scientists who harp on statistical representation of knowledge as the mantra of intellectual acuity. The question is: Are social scientists using statistical methods as a shield to hide their inability to communicate effectively what they discover? Let me not be mistaken. I am not defending researchers with a phobia for tables, graphs, and formulae. My concern is that most of that is unnecessary effort to complicate communication since ultimately, they have to explain the same in discourse. Nevertheless, there is a lot to be gained by applying some of the methods they use to interpretate data, especially coding which is applicable to content analysis. There are several ways in which coding can be applied effectively in the analysis of texts recorded during oral literature fieldwork. Coding, as Glaser and Strauss explain, is paradigmatic of the "constant comparative method" of grounded theory and qualitative data analysis. Its four-step analytic process consists of: comparing units of meaning across categories for inductive category coding; refining categories; "delimiting the theory" by exploring relationships and patterns across categories; and integrating data to write theory (Glaser and Strauss 1974, 105). Grounded theory is a form of latent structure analysis, which reveals the fundamental patterns in a substantive area or a formal area (Glaser 2002, 4).

Grounded theory suits the quest of oral literature fieldworkers because they are participant observers who never go out with highly-developed theories to test. The researcher employs ethnomethodology, which enables one to approach the community with an open mind and closely capture the performances, their own views about the performances, and their articulation of their situations from their own perspective. Within the grounded theory framework, fieldwork methodology develops during data collection. The theory resists any attempt to be limited to a researcher's preconceived research design. In this way, fieldwork in oral literature is able to capture data and indigenous theory of criticism based on the source community's evaluative standards. Grounded theory, by liberating meaning creation, falls directly within postmodernism.

According to *Merriam-Webster On-line Dictionary*, post-modernism refers to a theory that involves a radical reappraisal of modern assumptions about culture, literature, identity, history, or language. It represents a departure from modernism which encouraged a break with classical and traditional forms. To an extent, postmodernism is a return to the classical and traditional forms, not to celebrate them with nostalgia, but to salvage them from obscurity and to enrich contemporaneous thinking for alternative meaning creation.

As a theory that represents a radical shift in thought, postmodernism is associated with thinkers like Roland Barthes, Michel Foucault, Jacques Derrida, and Jacques Lacan. The theory re-conceptualizes the self as de-centred – as having no fixed centre or stable identity. It demolishes the canons and returns voice to the previously de-voiced segments of the society. It mistrusts the text as sacrosanct and offers alternative platforms through textualization, contextualization, en-textualization, inter-textuality, de-contextualization, re-contextualization and hypertext. Derrida, for instance, questions whether any cultural texts can have intrinsic authority or canonical status as accounts of "truths" about the phenomenal world. Derrida's approach to philosophic and literary "deconstruction" queries whether all texts comprise a dynamic play of "difference" which necessarily renders them polysemous (Baker and Luke 1991).

Post-modernism, with its promise of freedom and dissolution of boundaries, has liberated the former "other" but also created new dilemmas. It has paradoxically promoted globalization at the macro level while precipitating disintegration at the micro-level:

> With the relative weakening of the traditional nation-state, with the growth of multiculturalism and multiethnicism, with the increasing migration of peoples, the identity of many of the more important capitals and entrepots on the world map of culture has changed. ...Indeed, the entire topography of cultural expression has changed profoundly, on the one hand globalizing our access to artistic funds, but on the other intensifying the sense of place, region and ethnicity, as different groups break free of the cultural traditions and norms of the nation-state or the imperial system to assert more positive and independent identities. (Bradbury, 772)

The quest for identity by formerly marginalized groups, as Bradbury correctly observes, has metamorphosed into nationalism which manifests itself in ethnic, confrontational, and separatist in orientation. It has given the freedom it promised but denied the "other", the requisite responsibility that goes with the new freedoms. I have demonstrated this in Soyinka's argument against perceived theoretical colonialism. This has led to increased fragmentation and tribalism at the local level. In oral literature, sensitivity to ethnic identities has led to agitation for autonomy, violence, and exclusion of the "new other," even in theorization. It has created a new ground for queer theory which questions the notion that identities like tribe, clan, and women, straight, gay, and other minorities are homogenous and fixed. The queer theory, for example, contests generalizations because the characteristics assumed to be common are not shared by all members of the said group. The theory was originally associated with groups like feminists, lesbians, and homosexuals, but its tenets go beyond the interests of these specific groups to challenge what is considered normal, legitimate, and dominant in all spheres. It is a contest between "positionality" and the normative. In this respect, queer theory shares affinity with the postmodernist theoretical inclinations. Oral literature, therefore, has a rich field of theory to borrow from to promote scholarship in the discipline.

This chapter reveals that the study of oral literature in Africa has the potential to move away from the lack of theoretical audacity which Soyinka mentioned three decades ago, to critical praxis. It is learning to rediscover not only what Brown and Sidney refer to as "its own theoretical and pedagogical legs" (3), but also its epistemological foundation. It is also moving away from polarization that has characterized text and context diatribe to promote a dialogic engagement that balances academic concerns with aesthetic elements alongside social responsibility. In this new paradigm, theory is no longer allowed to guide fieldwork; instead, researchers either compel theory to work for them or they discard existing theories and engage in theory creation through grounded theory. For this to be realized, fieldworkers must confront the politics of field research boldly instead of denying that their activities are influenced by subjective decisions.

Methodology in Oral Literature

Oral literature fieldworkers do realise that one of the major challenges in the planning, and implementation of any research project is lack of clarity about several issues which are critical for the success of the study. Fieldworkers are never initially sure about what they are looking for, where they are likely to find answers to their questions, how to go about collecting relevant data, duration of the study, ethical considerations and who to involve in the study. Research methodology is meant to provide coherent answers to these questions. Other questions that fieldwork methodology elucidates are: Why undertake the study? What is the research problem? What kind of data is required? Why go to the field? Why select a particular location? How many research assistants are needed and for how long? And which are the appropriate methods or instruments for collecting the required data?

Finnegan, reflecting on the dilemma a researcher faces, suggests that methodology is about making choices that can lead to the realisation of the objectives of the study. For instance, a fieldworker must decide on, 'Whether to choose the best performers, or include a range of 'good' and 'bad' ones; whether to look for what is, or appears to be, 'old', 'traditional' or 'pure', or 'the current practices' (Finnegan 1992, 58). Methodology is supposed to respond to these and several other questions I am unable to exhaustively enumerate here.

Lack of clarity in the research process precipitates fear and excitement at the same time. It creates fear of the unknown which often scares young scholars from venturing into the jungle of fieldwork. At the same time, lack of clarity accelerates excitement in adventurous go-getters driven by curiosity to know. In this chapter, I do not pretend to provide answers to the plethora of questions that pop up in a researcher's head as he or she faces the unknown. Instead, I make the questions clearer so that a researcher is not taken by surprise when the research process demands certain answers. Research methodology provides credible and consistent answer to such questions.

A functional research methodology wraps up the study into a tidy whole with many of the critical questions answered. Methodology does not stop at providing answers to questions bothering a researcher, it also generates new questions that eliminate ambiguity about the knowledge the researcher is seeking. I consider a fieldworker's fear of the unknown rational, necessary and beneficial, when recognised early and managed well. It ensures caution and thoroughness at the planning stage of research methodology. To make the first and bold step of facing the field with its multiple and unpredictable questions and challenges, a fieldworker needs confidence that with proper planning, everything will work out well. It is research methodology, therefore, that imbues a fieldworker with confidence that research procedures and processes are controlled, logical and are insulated from personal biases or misguided enthusiasm.

Peter Clough and Cathy Nutbrown in their book *Research Methodology for Students* declare that "Research is methodology" (31). This powerful metaphor captures the centrality of methodology in a research enterprise. The term methodology refers to the processes, principles and procedures by which we approach problems and seek answers. In other words, the term refers to how one conducts research. Methodology is not purely objective, it is subjectively objective since the methodological procedures used are often influenced by the researcher's assumptions, interests and goals. Research methodology, can at best be described as a science of studying how the research is done scientifically. It elucidates the various steps adopted by a researcher in studying a research problem along with the logic behind them (Kothari, 10).

One may not be conscious of it, but a researcher is always engaged in a tacit struggle with the self to make methodological decisions that may lead to the achievement of the objectives of the study. The characteristic purpose of a research methodology is, therefore, to indicate not how such appeared to be "the best method available for the given purposes of the study, but how and why this way of doing it was unavoidably required by the context and purpose of this particular enquiry" (Frankfort-

Nachmias, C. and David Nachmias, 17). Methodology persuades the reader of the unavoidable triangular connection between the research questions, the methods used to operationalise the data so generated and the research findings. The purposes of the study determine the methodology and design of the research. In addition, it is the task of the methodology to uncover and justify research assumptions as far as practicably possible, in order to locate the claims which the research makes within the traditions of enquiry that use it. Methodological grounding and frankness in oral literature research is critical for the growth of the discipline because in their absence, there is a potential risk of reporting the discovery of knowledge that either already exists or does not emanate from the data analysed.

Methodology and Oral Literature Research

Research methodology that is sound and consistent makes a study scientific. Lastrucci C. L (1967) in *The Scientific Approach: Basic Principles of the Scientific Method,* contends that methodology conscious approach to fieldwork encourages a rigorous, impersonal mode of procedure dictated by the demands of logic and objective procedure (7). Literary scholars have for a long time suppressed the idea that oral literature is multidisciplinary and benefits immensely from developments in linguistics, religious studies, philosophy, anthropology, sociology and history (Wasamba 2007, 143). The policy of 'literary protectionism' extended to research methodology, where professors of literature often encouraged their students to be wary of research methodologies used by social scientists and other disciplines as they may dilute literariness of the discipline. I contest this conservative approach to scholarship because the reluctance of oral literature fieldworkers to experiment with research regimes in related disciplines significantly contributes to the marginalisation of the discipline, more so in Qualitative Data Analysis (QDA) discourse. Consequently, it has been argued that the integrity of the literary research data and their subsequent analyses cannot be verified because they are impressionistic and therefore, unscientific (Hymes, vii).

While terms like "impressionistic" and "unscientific" have been (mis)used by social scientists and 'natural scientists' to downgrade research in humanities, it cannot be denied that literature relies heavily on qualitative data and therefore stands to benefit a lot from the developments in QDA methods. Whenever the 'scientific' approach to research is mentioned, it is normally misunderstood to refer to studies by mainstream physical, biological and social scientists. Scientists from humanities are normally excluded because they allegedly cannot demonstrate their methods well. This is quite misleading because a scientific method to research implies a logical and systematic mode, free from personal bias or prejudice regardless of whether a scientist is from humanities, social sciences or 'hard' sciences. Embracing QDA approaches can revolutionise oral literature scholarship in the same way the introduction of stylistics upgraded literary criticism.

Stylistics is a category of applied linguistics dedicated to the study of style in texts, especially in literary works. Stylistics, as a bridge between literature and linguistics, is a theory that aims at validating intuitions through detailed empirical analysis. Katie

Wales in *A Dictionary of Stylistics* explains that stylistics contributes to 'objective' analysis of texts "in the sense of being methodical, systematic, empirical, analytical, coherent, accessible, retrievable and consensual" (Wales 2001, p. 373). A section of the literary fraternity initially resisted its application arguing that it is mathematical and makes a literary critic a captive of linguistic objectivity. While it is true that stylisticians concern themselves with minute details of grammar, lexis, phonology, prosody, meaning, as well as with the wider issues of deviation from the norm in their analysis of literary data, ultimately, "they must relate their analysis of the linguistic features to the consideration of content value and aesthetic quality in art," which grounds them in literature (Ngara, 12).

Oral literature research, as explained in the introductory chapter, concentrates on performances which are mainly qualitative. Means of documenting the performances and ensuing interviews are writing, memory, recording voices, filming or taking still pictures. It is seldom that an oral literature fieldworker employs tools like a questionnaire or other quantitative survey instruments common in social science research. As students of culture, oral literature researchers constantly strive to learn from their research environment by seeking detailed explanations, commentaries and reminiscences. Consequently, they need tools appropriate to their task in order to gather information relevant to the research topic. The conventional methods of collecting information are many. They include surveys, case studies, life histories and observation. For instance, using an interview schedule, informal conversation or participation, a fieldworker asks selected informants or oral artists questions about themselves, their lives, philosophies and performances, while at the same time observing what goes on in the community with his or her own eyes. The fieldworker usually tapes the interview session and takes notes as well. There is always a strong desire to maintain 'hygiene' in research. This is achieved by indicating clearly that researchers took steps to separate themselves from the objects they were studying.

The job of research methods, strictly speaking, is to 'hold apart' researchers and their objects, so that we can tell the difference between them. Methods do not tell us what is being researched; they do not even describe the study. All they tell us is the circumstances under which the researcher met the product of research. Furthermore, methods seek to provide a guarantee that the researcher and object are distinct from each other. Using the analogy of mechanics with their toolboxes, they cannot choose a wrong spanner to fix a mechanical problem. They will always pick the most appropriate tool from the toolbox to efficiently handle the task at hand. Research methods are, therefore, tools that we select from the fieldwork toolbox and use as need arises. This implies that methods only arise in the service of specific needs and purposes in a research process and their usefulness fades away if and when these needs are met and these purposes fulfilled.

Students recording a performance in Namaga September 2007 *Picture by Peter Wasamba*

Observation Method

The methods popularly employed by oral literature fieldworkers are observation and interviewing. Observation as a method of data collection is usually laid-back, involving recording and interpretation of what is observed. Observation is subjective because the sense one makes of what was observed depends on the person who participates in the observation. It is on account of some of the shortcomings of observation as a method of collecting information that Malinowski, one of the founding fathers of modern anthropology based on field research, formulated the famous concept of participant observation. In this context, the fieldworker participates in whatever the people do while at the same time, observing what they do, how and when. In field research, the primary sources of data are what people say and do. Researchers may record the behaviour they observe by writing notes, tape recording, and on occasion photographing or videotaping. In some cases when the researcher's identity and purpose are known to the observed, recording can be done on the spot, during the event. In most cases, however, the researcher wants members of the group to forget they are being observed so that their behaviour and interaction remain neutral.

Due to the limitations of the complete participant observer, a number of researchers especially university students at the beginning of their research careers opt for the participant as an observer approach. Researchers inform the group being studied before hand that they are visitors to the place on a research mission. That they intend to stay for a given duration documenting some aspects of the society's indigenous knowledge. That they would want the community to participate in a given way and that they beg for permission to be allowed in and be supported to achieve set research objectives. Participant observation creates the need for a face-to-face conversation with informants known as interviewing.

Structured and Unstructured Interview Methods

Interview is a tool used to gather first-hand information from respondents in a research framework based on their ability to remember. Interview method in an oral literature fieldwork context requires a person known as the interviewer asking questions generally in a face-to-face contact to the other person or persons. A fieldworker chooses between two types of interviewing: structured or unstructured interview. The Structured Interview is a data collection methodology that involves a standard set of questions asked in the same manner and order by a researcher. For example, when doing research, a researcher may interview participants instead of asking them to fill out a questionnaire. Experience shows that this method usually records a higher response rate. This is because in normal circumstances, it adds a human face with a personal touch to research. It enables a researcher to connect with a respondent in a more productive way. People are more likely to answer oral questions verbally during interviews rather than fill out a questionnaire that could be several pages long, boring and at times vague. Structured Interview method employs highly standardised techniques of recording. The interviewer follows a rigid procedure laid down in asking questions in a form and order prescribed. It is helpful in gathering information on genres of oral literature in society, biographical information about informants and major changes that have taken place in compositions and performances.

The unstructured interviews, to the contrary, are characterised by flexibility in questioning. The interviews do not follow a system of pre-determined questions and standardised techniques of recording information. The interviewers are allowed much greater freedom to ask, in case of need, supplementary questions or at times they may omit certain questions if the situation so requires. They may even change the sequence of questions. They have relatively greater freedom while recording the responses to include some aspects and exclude others. Unstructured interview demands deep knowledge and greater skill on the part of the interviewer.

To be a good interviewer, you need to learn how to ask focused questions and get rich information. You also need to be a good listener. Key to asking good questions is to avoid asking questions that can be answered with either a "yes" or "no," and instead ask questions that involve explanation. These are called "open-ended" questions. Be prepared ahead of time with a list of questions, but don't feel that you need to stay with this list. Ask "follow-up" questions based on what the person actually answers, not what's next on your list. Before you interview someone, practice asking questions first with a partner. Get detailed information, listen well, and do not interrupt while informants are speaking.

Dealing with people can be a daunting task because of the fear of the unexpected. The anticipation of the unfamiliar, coupled with a strong desire to manipulate circumstances to favour the desired goals of the study at times compels a fieldworker, in a positive way, to behave like a magician – covertly studying the background of the respondents and their psychology from neighbours or local assistant to be adequately prepared for productive engagement in an interviewing session. It is important to note that, though they never state it explicitly, informants too, expect researchers to have some basic information about them that justifies their selection in to the sample. It becomes embarrassing if researchers are ignorant about their informants. It is helpful for researchers to go beyond the expected basic information on an informant to discover some guarded information, knowledge of which may help them manage interview processes productively. Researchers should manage this intelligence gathering carefully to avoid the charge of intruding into informants' private lives.

Fieldwork Design

Fieldwork design is part of fieldwork methodology. An oral literature fieldwork design is a conceptual roadmap which guides the implementation of the proposed study. A well designed research project provides for the collection of relevant evidence with minimal expenditure on personnel, time, and finances. In preparing a research design, one should consider the means of obtaining the information, availability, and skills of researchers and their staff (if any), availability of relevant research equipment, justification of the means of collecting information, time available for research and financial implications for the study. Having a well thought-out research design ensures that little things normally taken for granted in a fieldwork project are identified, itemised and sequentially slotted in their relevant places along the research chain before venturing into the field.

An outline below does not in any way represent a perfect example of what a research chain looks like; nevertheless, it provides a clear idea about some of the milestones in a fieldwork process that researchers need to consider at the planning stage. Under the milestones, I mention some of the activities that fieldworkers should engage in to make sure that the research meets set objectives and quality standards. The key phases are:

laying down the infrastructure for fieldwork; conducting the actual fieldwork and post fieldwork activities.

Fieldwork Preparatory Phase

This is a critical phase in any research undertaking. The activities to be accomplished may look simple and even common sense, but with serious ramifications should any be skipped or neglected for lack of foresight. In this phase, the following activities should get attention:

- Review of relevant literature in the fields of folklore, oral literature, history, anthropology, linguistics, cultural studies and preparing a working bibliography.
- Identifying the research problem or topic (genre) and formulating research questions or problems on it.
- Writing the *research* (*project*) proposal which includes but not limited to the following: title of the project, short description or statement of the problem, objectives (goals) significance, limitation of the study, literature review, methods of research, research plan (tentative) and estimated cost of the project; if necessary one can prepare definition of basic or major terms and concepts to be used in the project.
- Developing tentative instruments for data collection such as interview schedule to gather or collect the various genres of oral literature targeted.
- Preparing tentative research budget.
- Selecting the research site and conducting a preparatory visit to the field.
- Getting administrative permission to conduct research at the selected site.

- Identifying and inducting research assistants.
- Pre-testing fieldwork instruments on the selected participants.
- Preparation of a tentative timetable (calendar) of the year or the seasons.
- Agreeing with the field assistants on the convenient dates for the actual fieldwork.
- Analysis of the data from the pilot study and revision of the instruments.
- Adjusting the budget and securing funds.
- Personal and psychological preparations of the researcher and assistants.
- Gathering maps and learning basic vocabulary of the local language.
- Buying the necessary field equipment for recording interviews, conversations, local ceremonies, performances and biographies.
- Getting important travel documents such as tickets, visa, and letter of cooperation or recommendation from a concerned authority. This can be obtained from University Research Institutes or Embassies.
- Buying medicines, vaccinations and preparing first aid kits.
- Prepare tokens for the host community and the informants.
- Departure: travelling to the research site (journeying to the community, country of the field research).

Fieldwork Phase

After a good preparation, a researcher is mentally and logistically ready to conduct fieldwork. In this phase, a researcher needs to:

- Enter quietly into the research site on the appointed day.

- Be ready to deal with the "field welcome" on the first few days or weeks in a strange environment: curiosity, confusion, attitudes of the local people, food and language problems.
- Pay courtesy call on the administrative officer and recognized community leadership in charge of the research site.
- Explain the purpose of the research and the fact that they have come to live among the community members to study their language, history, culture and poetic traditions among other areas of interest.
- Do not be too academic in the field. Take time to travel around, visiting localities, get to know the local people and find other potential field assistants, interpreters, translators and friends.
- Conduct general observation of the area and the local people by meeting elders, renowned persons, local chiefs and identify major local activities like harvesting seasons, sporting events, ceremonies, feasts, etc.
- Enlist the support of local assistants (earlier identified) in sampling.
- Test recording equipment for serviceability.
- Learn or improve on the local language; such as basic words and vocabularies useful for greeting forms, conversations, interviews, etc.
- Prepare a list of major performance occasions and try to select potential informants (local historians, public figures, singers/poets, narrators).
- Conduct research as quietly as possible based on the designed methodology.
- Make necessary appointments with the selected informants and other events organizers in the community.

- Attend important cultural, economic or political activities of the local people such as rituals, public gatherings, celebrations, festivals, initiation ceremonies; visit to sacred areas: shrines, churches, mosques, etc.
- Establish good friendship with selected persons or families in the villages.
- Employ observation, participation and intensive use of recordings.
- Conduct informal interviews and group discussions.
- Attending and recording live performances of major local events.
- Recording biographies of respected story tellers, singers, narrators.
- Taking pictures (with prior permission) of people, informants, performances, landscape, sacred places, etc., keeping diaries and field notes, carefully.
- Sharpening techniques and tactics: flexibility, patience and careful observation especially, while interviewing and approaching the local artists.
- Constantly reflecting on the progress based on the set objectives: How long can we stay? Have we collected sufficient material? What are the necessary adjustments required?
- Play the tapes briefly to the informants to confirm the recording.
- Take down correct contacts of the respondents for future correspondence
- Thank sincerely all those who have participated in the study.
- Observe the principle of reciprocity. Offer modest material or monetary tokens which is culturally appropriate.

- Leave the field quietly with the promise to return to the community.

Post-Fieldwork Phase

The last phase of any fieldwork, like the preparatory phase can be tricky. If not handled with care, all the effort and resources invested in the project may crumble due to inability to manage abundant success or control gnawing shortcomings at the tail-end of research. At the end of fieldwork, a researcher should consider the following:

- Plan the departure from the research site carefully.
- Leave a lasting positive impression so that your hosts look forward to receiving you again.
- Leave the field as quietly as you walked in.
- Analyze the data collected when the fieldwork experience is still fresh.
- Transcribe recorded texts (songs, chants, poems) and field notes.
- Translate and analyze the texts contextually, structurally and thematically.
- Listen to recordings repeatedly and cross check interviews and discussions.
- Prepare the final results: write theses; publish articles, books, and monographs, write conference papers, participate at seminars, workshops.
- Prepare audio and video (multimedia CD-ROMs), videos; digitize the recorded materials (data) based on original field notes, photos, texts, sound.
- Share the information with the host community.

- Document, preserve and archive data: in University Libraries, Archives or Documentation Centres systematically.
- Update data (additional field materials), contacts with former informants, friends, field assistants. Conduct further research: make documentary films, organize exhibitions, workshops, group excursions.
- Send copies of photos, research results, publications to local libraries and academic institutions; or even to key informants; and field assistants.
- Prepare a field research report.
- Organize another study to address gaps identified by the initial research.
- The cycle continues.

The three phases discussed above flow in a linear progression. Though there may be cases of minor overlaps where one phase ends and another one begins, no phase can replace or run parallel to another. The activities implemented within each one of them, nevertheless, do not have to follow the order in which they are stated, they can be reorganised hierarchically based on a researcher's specific situation. As any careful researcher will predictably notice, the activities within each of the phases are neither exhaustive nor conclusive. They can be modified through inclusion or exclusion to achieve the desired results of a specific study. It is important that researchers anticipate these phases and plan for them. Fieldwork does not allow for haphazard thinking and unstructured interventions. The procrastinatory creed of, "we will cross the bridge when we get there," has no place at all in fieldwork methodology. This should not be misinterpreted to mean that fieldworkers have to be unreasonably inflexible to the contingencies in the field. It simply insists that even contingencies are anticipated and accommodated within the methodology. Other emergencies are dealt with based on researcher's intelligence, commonsense and instinct for survival. For example, when in the middle of a performance in the village, two members of the audience who are drunk disagree on the aesthetic value of a performance and begin to fight it out viciously with crude weapons, a researcher cannot refer to the predesigned methodology to decide on what to do: whether to shield the artist from possible injury, face the armed fighters and plead for peace; or grab the recording equipment and take flight to safety. All depends on the ability to make quick and appropriate judgement for self preservation. In any case, nobody goes to the field to die. A researcher is neither a martyr nor a Japanese *kamikaze*.

Qualities of a Consummate Fieldworker

An ideal fieldworker has superior qualities that many researchers may not have. At the same time, fieldworkers are human beings with various character limitations. It is imperative that a field researcher conducts self appraisal to know his or her strengths and weaknesses as a community worker. In my assessment, a fieldworker should exhibit at least 70 per cent of the qualities of a good fieldworker to succeed in a research project. A good oral literature fieldworker should be a man or woman:

- Good in rapport creation
- Modest
- Sensitive to the cultures of other people
- Adventurous

- Analytical
- Open-minded
- Tolerant
- Well read in the area of study
- Competent in the use of research equipment
- Appreciative
- Presentable

It is safe to begin from the premise that researchers need the community. It is therefore incumbent upon researchers to conduct themselves in a manner that endears them to the community. Due to many studies going on, especially, in poor neighbourhoods, the population is fatigued and will most likely turn the request for another interview down. Research among the poorer sections of the society has of late been flatteringly referred to as poverty tourism. This has a negative connotation of laughing at a people's genuine struggle to hang on to life in nearly impossible circumstances. The way in which researchers present themselves will determine whether they are accepted or rejected. Researchers should desist from assuming that the villagers will be so happy to have them around since they look expensive, modern and speak with a foreign accent. At the same time, a researcher should not visit poor informants shabbily dressed as a way of expressing solidarity with them. They will know you are faking poverty without experiencing its demeaning pathology. The qualities of a good researcher outlined above are therefore important. They are obviously not conclusive. I encourage you to extend the list further because each community will have its standards of decency, integrity and hospitality. Researchers too are also not homogenous. Some are strong in some traits and weak in others. Awareness of their strengths and weaknesses enables them to make necessary adjustments to achieve research goals.

Fieldwork Participants

Fieldwork in oral literature is not only multi-disciplinary; it is also a multi-task activity. It requires the cooperation of several players to succeed. The tendency, nonetheless, has been to attribute all success to only one person – the lead researcher, and failure to acknowledge the 'other' invisible players. The current thinking in research theory challenges this traditional domineering notion of fieldwork. Democratization of fieldwork has opened up space to hitherto voiceless players in data collection process that has led to calls for the inclusion of their voices and interests in the definition of the project. The new thinking also insists that lead researchers remove what Rosaldo terms their "mask of innocence" to confront the asymmetrical power relations with which their work is complicit (Horner, 16).

Alcoff M. Linda correctly observes in *The Problem for Speaking for Others* that speaking for others, especially when they are present and can speak for themselves, "is arrogant, vain, unethical and politically illegitimate" (97). By insisting on the inclusion of all players in a fieldwork project, the new fieldwork regime reconstitutes the original fieldwork family. I use the term fieldwork family to refer to participants who comprise a research team. Like a family, the team's success depends on how each member complements the activities of the whole. The head of the fieldwork family is the lead researcher. Other members of the family are research assistants, field assistants, respondents, and fieldwork support staff such as drivers, accounts officers and medical personnel. Like the head of the family, the lead researcher has power, vision, resources and wherewithal to ensure the success of the project, but without harnessing the potential in each member of the family, his or her efforts may come to naught.

It is preferable to have one person as a lead researcher in charge of fieldwork activity. In a university environment, the specialist in oral literature, linguistics, sociology, anthropology, cultural studies or oral history heads the research team. Lead researchers do not work alone. They assemble teams of research assistants together with the fieldwork support group. Essential qualities of an oral literature fieldwork team leader are:

- Academic grounding in oral literature and the neighbouring disciplines.
- Hands-on experience in conducting fieldwork in various situations.
- Multi-disciplinary methodological and theoretical exposure
- Organisational prowess.
- Financial discipline.
- Enthusiasm and genuine commitment to the project.
- Good local and international contacts.
- Good communication skills.

Lead researchers are expected to do some initial research into the subject of the project, and find out the level of knowledge available in the area; draw up the provisional budget and timetable for the work; ensure research assistants have appropriate equipment; identify potential informants, and ensure data collection proceeds as planned. Further, they are tasked to equip research assistants with interviewing skills; monitor fieldwork progress and offer necessary support. In addition, team leaders are supposed to conduct periodic review meetings as deemed appropriate and supervise transcription, translation, analysis and interpretation. The effectiveness of a team leader is crucial to the project's progress and ultimate success, hence the need for a check-list like the one outlined below.

Lead Researcher's Check-list

1. Identification of the Fieldwork Site: In deciding on the location where the data collection will take place, the lead researcher needs to think through some of these issues:

- The research topic
- Geography of the location
- Population density
- Infrastructure
- Language
- Security situation
- Local administration
- Distance from the researcher's station
- Availability of health facilities
- Availability of supportive local assistants
- Contacts with researchers who have worked in the same locality

- Availability of material on previous research activities in the area

2. Transport and communication

- Identify appropriate and reliable transport to, within, and from the research location
- Identify other means of transport in the field to complement road transport like the use of canoes, donkeys, bicycles and trekking
- Prepare research assistants to be ready to travel in difficult terrain
- Where possible ensure access to telephone and internet services

3. Accommodation in the field

- Use local assistants to identify accessible, affordable, quiet, clean and secure accommodation
- Have adequate budget for accommodation and subsistence for they are likely to be higher than what was originally budgeted
- Book and reconfirm reservations for accommodation before going to the field
- Where possible, encourage research assistants to voluntarily share rooms for security, cost reduction and bonding
- The lead researcher should stay at the same facility or very close

4. Plan for adequate supervision during data collection

- Assess the magnitude of the data to be collected
- Confirm the number of research assistants engaged for fieldwork and their grounding in research methodology

- Consider the number of fieldwork sites and their proximity to the station
- The duration of fieldwork
- Assess the terrain of the research location and plan transport well
- Decide on the number of researchers needed to guide students in the field
- Know the weather patterns in the locality and have contingency plans

5. Arrangements for local assistants

- The number of assistants required
- Gender and age composition of the local assistants
- Their previous experience in research
- Ability to ensure neutrality
- Have an agreement on the expected compensation before engagement

6. Clothing and footwear requirements

- Study the weather, religious and other cultural issues in the research location and advice research assistants on clothing and footwear requirements, before departing to the field

7. Arrangements for data collection equipment

- Identify research methods and instruments required for data collection
- Ensure availability and serviceability of the field work equipment before the commencement of the study

- Let research assistants demonstrate competence in the use of data collection equipment before they venture into the field
- Encourage the use of high quality machines
- Carry extra machines to safeguard against disappointment in case one fails abruptly
- Train research assistants on trouble shooting in case of equipment malfunction

Field Research Assistants

These tasks make the lead researchers principal players in any fieldwork expedition. The decisions they make before, during and after fieldwork have the potential of completely altering the direction, pace and results of the study. Although the terminologies are applied differently in other studies, in this book, I use the terms 'lead researcher,' team leader, and the 'principal researcher' interchangeably.

The principal researcher, depending on the scope of the study may opt to collect data alone. However, in many situations, the researcher sees wisdom in recruiting technical staff with capacity to be trained to assist in data collection. These women and men are often referred to as research assistants. They are expected to apply the research instruments with the efficiency that rivals that of the lead researcher. The quality of personnel recruited depends on the type of research, location and duration.

Qualitative research demands that research assistants be well educated, possibly with postgraduate degrees, due to the demand for refined interviewing skills. Quantitative research which relies mainly on the administration of questionnaires may only need a first degree holder, and sometimes even high school graduates. Research assistants can be students under training or applicants recruited through a competitive process. They are trained on the administration of research tools before being contracted to meet the set targets. Good research assistants should be grounded on research methodology, good at the administration of research instruments, rich in fieldwork experience, patient, adventurous, and ready to learn. They should have the capacity to carry on with the research to its logical end should something unexpected make the lead researcher indisposed.

New researchers entering the field should expect some kind of 'escort politics' in relation to how outsiders are managed by host communities. In fieldwork situations, it is useful for the researcher to select 'good' local contact persons (Gokah, 71). The problem is that it may not be easy knowing a 'good' local assistant, especially when you are a visitor in a community. People have the tendency to perform 'being good' to visitors only to revert to their initially concealed 'bad habits' in the middle of the project. With all the risk involved, a fieldworker still needs a local assistant in order to operate smoothly in the field. I have noticed in my previous research engagements that local assistants can innocently hijack the fieldwork project if not politely kept under close check. They try to arrange the fieldwork itinerary to suit their interests and decide on the informants a researcher can or cannot visit, without regard to the researcher's budget and sampling methods. At times they even negotiate tokens to be given to informants they prefer way beyond what the budget allows.

Field Local Assistant

A local assistant is purely a host and a guide to the researcher in the field. In many cases, a field assistant is a respected man or woman who is a resident in the host community. For a successful fieldwork, local assistants should be carefully selected, trained and briefed because they may not be well educated but very resourceful in rapport creation, mobilisation of respondents and communicating research agenda in a way understood by local people. They should be honest, sincere, hardworking, and impartial. In addition, they must possess the necessary practical experience in fieldwork within the community. Local assistants in an oral literature fieldwork project are expected to among other tasks: adopt the researcher to facilitate acceptance by other community members; offer security tips to the researcher; introduce the researcher to individual informants admired in the society for their eloquence and knowledge of oral tradition; demonstrate deep interest in mastering the tradition of their people and must be willing to remain politically neutral for the entire period of fieldwork.

There is a tendency to concentrate on the technical wing of a fieldwork project without giving due attention to the operational wing of the project. The technical wing comprises the lead researcher, research assistants and on rare occasions, local assistants. The operational wing of a fieldwork project consists of the research driver, an accountant and a wellness officer. A cursory review of fieldwork literature reveals paucity of information on the contribution of drivers, accountants and doctor/nurses to the success or failure of research projects. These players sometimes make great sacrifices to make the project a success while in other cases, they are a great hindrance to the study.

Research Driver

For a group fieldwork one of the key players is the research driver. They are in charge of making sure that the research team gets to the research locations and return to the station safely. A driver taking a team out for fieldwork must be experienced in basic research etiquette which includes ethical behaviour, punctuality, ingenuity and resilience. I had an opportunity to conduct research in 2005 with a driver called John Ngunjiri of Netherlands Development Organisation (SNV-Kenya), who was so resourceful that with time - since we were only two people in the field for close to two months - a strong professional and social bond developed between us. He performed the roles of a research driver, research assistant, field assistant and a bodyguard, all at the same time. He assisted me more than the local people who had been identified for support assignments by the client organisation. He was proficient in four local languages used by four ethnic communities in the research location namely Pokot, Bukusu, Marakwet and Turkana and could switch codes with amazing ease. Further, he was conversant with the geography and socio-political dynamics of the region based on his previous fieldwork driving expeditions. The resourcefulness of my driver elevated him to a respected local assistant who always offered timely advice before interviews. With time, the hierarchy between the driver and the researcher collapsed, we remained colleagues, and above all, brothers. There has never been an exciting fieldwork experience closer to this one in my research career.

l have also had my fair share of disappointments with drivers who, at times, refuse to work at odd hours, disable the vehicle mechanically to frustrate the study, decline to take legitimate instructions, intrude into interviewing sessions, drive under the influence of alcohol and engage in pilferage of money meant for fuel and maintenance of the research vehicle. On one occasion, a driver declined to take a research assistant to a certain village to interview an artist. He argued that the road to that village was too narrow for a big vehicle, which was not true since he had never gone to that village. I weighed all options which included disciplining him in the field and concluded that acrimony would distract the team from the fieldwork objective. I decided to hire a taxi for the research assistant at an extra cost. At the end of that particular fieldwork, I decided never to use the particular driver again, a promise I have kept to date.

On another occasion, a driver indulged in a local brew called *kaada* among the Turkana in Lodwar, a town close to the Kenya-Southern Sudan border, the whole night on the eve of our planned departure the following morning. The following day, while driving back to our base, some 150 kms, he dozed off on the wheels overwhelmed by the mid-morning heat. I did not realise he was dozing because he had thick sun glasses on. The vehicle did a terrifying zig-zag on the road before veering off to the right side of the road dangerously. What saved us was the desert terrain and the high suspension of the vehicle. We nearly rolled. My terrifying yell woke him up. He struggled and managed to control the vehicle which was galloping over the stones and shrubs. This was one of the most scaring experiences of my life. I had not driven such a vehicle, but I had no choice. I persuaded him to hand over the car key and allow me to drive him which he reluctantly accepted. Thereafter, I allowed the driver to take a nap on the passenger's seat as I drove to our destination. I suspended the research until a professional driver was provided.

These experiences have taught me that a driver for research trips must be responsible, honest, intelligent, tolerant, adventurous and sociable. The power relations must be clearly defined so that the drivers know they must take orders from the lead researcher or any other researcher with delegated authority. The lead researcher should be friendly, human in dealing with the drivers but remain firm and diplomatic in discharging research duties. Do not starve the drivers or misuse them beyond the official call of duty such as frequently driving to private visits at night or spending most of your time in social places instead of conducting research. Good drivers normally study their superiors before misbehaving. They are always keen to know when they are being misused and will respond by defying orders which are illegitimate.

One way in which a lead researcher can reduce the challenges drivers face in the field is by ensuring that they board in the same facility with other researchers. This has been a challenge to me because the allowances drivers are entitled to, based on their job grades are quite low and they cannot afford the hotels where researchers reside. It has not been easy getting additional support for drivers from the sponsors due to rigid financial regulations. I have always negotiated discount rates for my drivers with the hotel management such that it becomes a condition for booking the facility. The approach ensures security for the vehicle and the drivers and their availability at short notice. I have since learnt that good hotels have provisions for drivers at no or minimal cost. But the lead researcher must ask for this concession.

It is assumed that any driver can take charge of field transport during research competently. This may not be the case. New drivers need to be trained on the basics of fieldwork so that they understand their supporting role early enough. This is because, as stated before, in fieldwork, intelligence, discipline, solidarity and punctuality are non-negotiable requirements. In addition, the driver must make sure the following items are in the vehicle: sport light with new batteries, jack and wheel change set, fuel can, spade, spare wheel, tow rope, water can and First Aid Kit. One may dismiss the above list as obvious and that any qualified driver would know better and that they are indispensible for any trip. Experience has taught me that in fieldwork, nothing is left to chance.

Many drivers only think about immediate concerns such as their per diems, availability of fuel and servicing the vehicle. They hardly think of the probable challenges and how to prepare for them. It is important that a researcher ensures that the vehicle is loaded with emergency tools before departing for the field. On one occasion, I was surprised to discover that a driver keen on getting his allowance drove the vehicle full of research assistants to the research site over 500kms away from the university knowing too well that he did not have enough money for fuel. The fuel that was available could not last for one day in the field and yet the research was to last seven days. I sent him back using public means at his own cost to go and look for fuel money. The university stepped in and organised for emergency fuelling in the field and a substitute driver to enable the study go on. These are some harsh decisions that one may be forced to make in the field.

Gender, driving and fieldwork also deserve mention. Gender discrimination has for a long time been practised in driving pools of research institutions, when it comes to the recruitment of drivers and deploying them on research assignments. The argument advanced is that women cannot stay away from their families for too long. Others have also argued that driving in the field is a male domain that women may not handle competently. The other reasoning which is never mentioned is that research driving has a good monetary reward that male drivers are not willing to share with women drivers. The University of Nairobi is not an exception in this debate. The percentage of women drivers in the entire organisation is less than 5 per cent.

Women are hardly considered as viable candidates for drivers' jobs because driving has been traditionally a man's domain. I have learnt that with proper training, encouragement and exposure to the field, women can make the competent fieldwork drivers. They are focused, courteous, time conscious and enjoy teamwork as opposed to male drivers who have several secondary interests besides driving. In interviewing women respondents, l learned that having a female driver also facilitates rapport and inspire local girls to go to school to get good jobs. In some of the villages visited, not many girls have gone to school. A woman driver is therefore an enigma. This should not be misinterpreted to mean all women drivers are good fieldworkers. I have also had disappointing cases. Some women drivers are too choosy in the field. They require exceptionally clean sleeping places and special food like what they take in their houses. Some are short tempered and easily get unreasonably irritable when work goes on for too long. The above observation cannot be used to exclude women drivers from fieldwork. They deserve a chance, encouragement and support, just like male drivers.

Fieldwork Accountant

Financial resources are critical for fieldwork. Incorporating the finance section of the sponsoring institution in the planning stages of fieldwork is unavoidable in ensuring timely and adequate   disbursement of research funds. In this regard, the lead researcher should liaise with the accounts section to ensure that the fieldwork budget is adequate and that funds are processed and disbursed in good time for the planned activities. There exists an undeclared cold-war between accounts personnel and fieldworkers. It is characteristic for accounts personnel to dispute nearly all budget lines for fieldwork. This is understandable considering that their work hardly takes them to the field. It is also predictable for researchers to get upset and hurl expletives whenever their budget lines are queried by accounts officers.

It boils down to attitude problem. I have often pitied my colleagues who have to idle along the corridors of accounts departments pleading for money applied for long before the day of departure to the field. In some sad cases, planned field trips have had to be cancelled or postponed on the day of the departure over misunderstandings that could have been addressed earlier. Such cases affect the morale of the researchers and reduce the research days. There is need for a truce. To help the accounts section, researchers should prepare realistic budgets that can be understood and justified by auditors based on the policy guidelines that control the use of funds in the sponsoring institutions. They should also include adequate explanation of the budget lines to put the auditors in the picture. Fieldwork budgets should include entitlements for the research team for subsistence and accommodation, the costs of equipment like recorders, tapes, batteries, stationary; the costs for fuelling and maintaining the research vehicle (it is assumed that institutions have vehicles and therefore do not have to hire transport) or return tickets; honoraria for research assistants, field assistants and respondents; fees for transcription and translation and contingency for unforeseeable expenses.

It has become a common practice to do cost-sharing in universities. It means that students going to the field shoulder part of the cost such as their accommodation, meals and research equipment. The university, on the other hand, provides transport, pays for the lecturer's subsistence, and allowances for local assistants and tokens for informants. The element of cost sharing should be handled with flexibility and compassion. I have had to support students who are quite promising as researchers but are not able to raise the matching funds to join the field work class. In a number of cases, fellow students have contributed to support some students who cannot pay for themselves. Such philanthropic gestures should be encouraged as they promote empathy and teamwork in the class. Thinking about finances is important even if one is sponsoring the study from personal sources because it is easy to forget a critical budget-line only to discover in the field that you need additional cash. The easy way for doing one's own budget is to list all the activities planned for fieldwork and then cost each item in order to arrive at the total sum required. Do not be generous in your budget because resources are limited. In the same vein, do not be stingy with the budget because making adjustments later on in the field may be too difficult and painful. A budget must be solid and realistic.

Fieldwork and Wellness

Health services departments also have a role to play in a fieldwork project. In an ideal situation, a trained health officer should accompany students or a large research team to the field. Nevertheless, due to shortage of staff and funds this may not be possible, especially when students going out for research are few. To equip researchers with skills in First Aid and how to dispense basic drugs for common ailments, the Health Services Department should in-service researchers and research assistants regularly on First Aid skills, how to dispense drugs for common ailments, and procedures for accessing proper medical care in case of emergency in the field. A standard First Aid Kit, according to the Kenya Red Cross Society, should have a minimum of the following contents:

Table 1: First Aid Kit Contents

	Items	Qty
1.	Adhesive dress strips	25
2.	Adhesive tape	1
3.	Blunt-sharp scissors	1
4.	Disposable face shield	1
5.	Disposable gloves	Several
6.	Eye pad	2
7.	Crepe bandage 10cm	1
8.	Crepe bandage 7.5 cm	1
9.	Crepe bandage 5cm	1
10.	Sterile gauze swaps	3
11.	Non adhesive dressing	3
12.	Safety pins	10
13.	Splinter forceps	1
14.	Sterile water 10ml	5
15.	Absorbent tissues	10
16.	Triangular bandages	3
17.	Wound dressing No. 8	2
18.	Wound dressing No 9	1
19.	Iodine 125ml	1
20.	Note book and pen	1
21.	Disposal tags	2
22.	Clinical thermometer	1
23.	Alcohol pre pad	1
24.	Crepe bandage 10cm	1
25.	Crepe bandage 7.5 cm	1

The Health staff should also undertake to periodically inspect the First Aid kit to remove the expired drugs and replenish the kit before every departure to the field. I was preparing to go to the field with students some time back when one of my colleagues walked into my office and offered to help with preparations. She chanced to inspect the First Aid Kit I had packed for the trip and was shocked to discover that nearly all the drugs inside had expired. I felt so embarrassed for not having thought about it, I could have poisoned my students and myself in the field without knowing. The danger was averted by that chance inspection. Though it is not mentioned publicly, it is important that awareness of HIV/AIDS prevention methods be revisited as part of the preparation for any fieldwork. Change of environment has a way of exciting desires that may expose researchers to various risks of infecting others or getting infected with the virus that causes AIDS. The disease is still a taboo in large parts of the world due to stigma associated with it. Fieldwork methodology must take on board HIV/AIDS awareness creation and prevention methods because as George Homan correctly puts it, research methodology "is a matter of strategy, not of morals" (330).

Literature Review and Sampling

Other methodological considerations that a fieldworker needs to anticipate are a thorough review of relevant literature, sampling techniques, rapport creation, interviewing process, field equipment, and the fieldwork setting. Review of literature relevant to a given study is a critical to examination, interpretation or evaluation of existing literature in order to establish the state of knowledge on a topic or subject selected for a detailed study. Reviewers of literature are keen to contextualize research in terms of what other enquirers have claimed as findings. A thorough review of literature relevant to an area of study is critical for a focused and productive fieldwork. Availability of literature is not limited to visiting one library or internet; it requires extensive search for literature over a period of time. There are two types of literature review that one needs to be conversant with: conceptual and empirical literature. The conceptual literature deals with the concepts and theories, while the empirical literature consists of studies made earlier which are similar to the one proposed. A researcher can conduct a productive literature review by looking at relevant journals, published or unpublished bibliographies, conference proceedings, earlier studies similar to the one at hand, World Wide Web and well-stocked libraries.

Sampling is one important research activity that oral literature fieldworkers have not been forthright in explaining. Whereas it is assumed that oral literature texts can be collected from almost anyone in the community, not every person is an expert oral artist or opinion leader. In deed, in every community, there are men and women, boys and girls, who by virtue of their socialisation, good memories, personal experiences, performance skills, careers, or particular roles, and responsibilities within a community, are considered more gifted in preserving oral texts, enriching them continuously and sharing them with the public through performances. This calls for a deliberate way of sampling to identify and interview these custodians of tradition. Sampling is a definite plan determined before data is actually collected from a given population. Some of the sample designs frequently applied in oral literature research are deliberate sampling and random sampling. Deliberate sampling, also known as purposive or non-probability sampling, involves a purposeful selection of the units to be analysed. Deliberate sampling comprises convenience sampling and judgement sampling. Convenience sampling refers to a situation where the elements are selected for inclusion in the sample based on ease of access. Judgement sampling is a scenario where, the researchers' judgement is used for selecting items which they consider as representative of the population. This is not to say that convenience and judgement sampling allow the researcher to operate in a haphazard or biased manner. The researchers' application of the above sampling design is normally informed by the research topic, informant's age, gender, profession, social status, religion, research assistant's opinion, community members' opinions, the nature of the terrain, the prevailing weather conditions, political climate at the time and the researcher's disposition.

Unless one is deliberately focusing on a particular sector, narrators should come from a range of ages, occupations, social backgrounds, and experiences. Most of them should be "ordinary" people who can speak about their own experiences, perceptions and concerns (Giving Voices, 18). The sampling approach I propose for oral literature fieldwork resonates to some degree with grounded theory's concept of theoretical sampling where the "process of data collection is controlled by the emerging theory, whether substantive or formal" (Bong, 19). Random sampling, on the other hand, is also known as chance sampling or probability sampling where each and every item in the population has an equal chance of inclusion in the sample and each one of the possible samples has the same probability of being selected. For example, we may choose to select 20 oral artists out of a 1000 through random sampling. We may name and number all the oral artists and then put the papers on the table and conduct a lottery. This method gives all oral artists identified equal opportunity of being selected. The only misgiving with this approach in oral literature research is that, one may not get a fairly representative data in terms of genres specialization, age, gender and interest in culture. In collecting oral texts from a given community, the researcher would be keen in recording the best artists in each category. This may not come out through random sampling. Random sampling presupposes uniformity among artists which is not always the case. The approach can only apply when one is using the ethnological approach which is based on the wrong assumption that oral narratives are easily composed and performed by any member of the society.

Rapport Building

Fieldworkers often dread the defining moment, that is, the first few minutes with the respondent: How do you find respondents to interview? How do you invite yourself into a respondent's humble dwelling? How do you interest them in your project so that they participate productively? These worries can be addressed through good rapport creation, which means, establishing relations with members of the host community for purposes of gathering useful research information. To gain entry and acceptance into a community, fieldworkers need to be friendly, patient, diplomatic and articulate in introducing themselves, the purpose of the research, why it is important for the community to get involved, duration and how the research findings are likely to impact on their lives. I have always instructed students to go to the field humbled by the fact that nobody out there is compelled to give them any information. Convincing respondents that a researcher is worthy of respect, time and trust, hence, becomes a litmus test for a methodologically conscious researcher. Some of the factors that influence gaining access into a community are gender, religion, race, age, ethnicity, level of education, money and terrain. The ease with which a fieldworker establishes relationships with members of a group depends to a large extent on the nature of the group and the skills of the researcher. In a well-balanced relationship, fieldworkers strive to maintain a consciousness and admiration for what they are and a consciousness and respect for what their informants are.

Rapport creation is a delicate stage in asserting one's presence in the field. I have noticed two tendencies that inhibit researchers from handling this phase smoothly. I refer to the extreme positions adopted by novice fieldworkers in rapport creation as either 'going native' or 'going ozone' in the field. Researchers 'go native' when, in a bid to let their differences with community members melt away, they over-identify with the community to the extent that they sink and get completely submerged into the community's ways such that their identity as researchers disappear. This can be observed in researchers drinking themselves silly in public, dressing shabbily and engaging in open casual relationships with local people of the opposite sex. While it is recommended that researchers adopt the ways of host communities, there are unstated boundaries that a researcher should not cross.

'Going ozone,' is the opposite of 'going native.' The term is derived from 'ozone layer' which refers to the layer in the earth's stratosphere at an altitude of about 10 km containing a high concentration of ozone, which absorbs most of the ultraviolet radiation reaching the earth from the sun. In fieldwork, going ozone is a metaphor for receding further away from the subjects of study. It means exaggerating the otherness of a researcher. Fieldworkers who go 'ozone,' are keen to amplify how unlike the respondents they are in terms of status and sophistication. This can be observed in a researcher's demeanour, dressing, walking, talking, eating and general attitude. Such behaviours may turn the community off and result in silent rejection or an open outrage because of the condescending attitude of the researcher. I remember participating in a field study in 1992 as an undergraduate student. The research site was among the Maasai of Namanga, which borders Tanzania. A number of female students in our group did not record performances. They argued that the research locale was stinking and full of houseflies. Consequently, their hands were too busy fending off houseflies to document performances. The two attitudes may cost a researcher valuable data. A researcher should maintain balance between 'going native' and 'going ozone.'

The fieldworker's attitude to those being studied is not only relevant but also critical for acceptance and learning. Hamish Hamilton's guideline in the preface to Goldstein's classic *A Guide*

for Fieldworkers in Folklore is worth considering. He contends
that fieldworkers:

> ....should never, in the heat of data collection, forget their humanist
> role. They are helping to interpret man to man – his beliefs, glories,
> dreams, and darknesses. If they adopt a patronizing attitude to
> what they are studying, they may well blind themselves to its real
> nature. And if they treat their informants purely as sources of
> information, to be taken up and discarded as occasion demands,
> they are in grave danger of losing more than their friendship. If ever
> an academic collector is tempted to proceed on the assumption
> that he/she 'knows' more about oral literature than his informants
> do, they'd be well advised to remember the wise words of A. N
> Whitehead: 'The self-confidence of learned people is the comic
> tragedy of civilization.' (Goldstein 1964: xi)

Constant awareness by fieldworkers of their humanist role, as
Hamilton suggests, can reduce the challenges researchers
encounter in unfamiliar locations. It also stops a researcher from
being a comical 'native' or an alienated 'elitist.'

Fieldwork Documentation

There are several ways to record the information collected in the
field. One may take notes, use an audio tape recorder, or a video
tape recorder, or simply rely on memory. Researchers recording
performances should:

- Practice and learn how to use the machines before going to the
  field;
- Use fresh batteries and new cassette tapes;

- Remember to place the microphone near the informant being interviewed;
- Use more than one camera and qualified personnel to operate them from different angles in case of video recording;
- Take detailed notes. It is a good idea to write a summary from observations while the interview is fresh in the mind, or the notes may not make sense later; and
- Keep field notes separate from notes containing personal observations.

Interview Method

An interview, is a time for fieldworkers to display the best of their skills. Whereas there is no set way of recording performances and conducting interviews, a guide to some of the steps in the interviewing process is helpful. Researchers should:

- Know the social calendar of the community and the daily routine of the potential respondents.
- Pay courtesy call on the potential respondent accompanied by local assistant.
- Explain clearly what the fieldwork is about, and what they expect from informants.
- Request politely for appointments to record performances and conduct interviews.
- Use common courtesies, such as addressing adults by their proper titles.
- Be punctual and prepared for the interviews.
- Seek permission to record the performances and to take pictures.

- Begin the interviews by recording identification of informants. A sample format could be: "This is _____ (researcher's name), and I am speaking with _____ (artist's name). We are in _____ (village, Ward, County), and today's date is _____.''

- Remember to listen keenly and to ask useful questions at the end of the performance.

- Start recording on side A of the tape and only turn over B if the same narrative flows over (for analogue tapes). When the interview formally comes to an end, the interviewer should declare, "end-of-interview".

- Use digital voice recorders to avoid challenges of analogue tapes. You will enjoy high quality recording, larger memory space, ease of transcription, and even in some cases translation.

- Never overstay the welcome and bore the hosts.

- Request the interviewees to sign release forms that explain the purpose of the interview and documents their permission to use the material.

- Relax and have some informal discussion with hosts if situation permits at the end of the interview.

- Request respondents to identify other artists respected locally for their accomplishments.

- Label tapes and cassette boxes while in the field.

- Offer an appreciation to the local participants depending on ability and material situations.

- Remember to thank the hosts.

- Leave the field as quietly as they came in.

- Send a 'thank you' note together with a few developed photos of the informants soon after returning to the research station.

- Stay in touch with the respondent through phone calls, mails and even greetings sent through other people.

Transcription and Translation

Let me revisit transcription and translation matters here. Oral literature source material is normally approached, used, and represented through expensive, time consuming and cumbersome transcription into text. Even when the enormous flattening of the meaning inherent in text reduction is recognized, transcription has seemed quite literally essential – not only inevitable, but something closer to 'natural.' The assumption in this near universal practice is that only in text can the material be efficiently and effectively engaged – text is easier to read, scan, browse, search, publish, display, and distribute. Audio or video documents, in contrast, inevitably have to be experienced in 'real time.' Even as we find ourselves trapped into transcription and translation, it is important to remind ourselves that "meaning inheres in context and setting, in gesture, in tone, in body language, in expression, in pauses, in performed skills and movements. To the extent that we are restricted to text and transcription, we will never locate such moments and meaning, much less have the chance to study, reflect on, learn from, and share them" (Frisch, 103).

What one needs to carry to the field may sound too obvious, but at the risk of being dismissed as trivial, I include some of them here so that one does not forget since it may be almost impossible to get some of the items in the field. When we list down what to carry for a meaningful oral literature fieldwork, we are guided by necessity and not comfort. The list will vary according to the project. A simple check-list for fieldworkers might include but not limited to the following items:

- Notebooks, pens, and pencils
- Camera, film, or digital medium and accessories as may be needed
- Audio or video recorder (battery-operated ones are useful); microphones; adequate number of fresh tapes, batteries and an extension cord
- Appropriate dresses and shoes
- Release forms
- Map of the area
- Administrative permission to conduct research in the area
- Legally acceptable identification document
- A portable computer
- Portable oral literature textbooks relevant to the study
- First aid kit well stocked with drugs for common ailments or dangers in the research location.
- Torch
- Mobile phone
- Adequate funds

It is common knowledge, especially in universities training students in ethnographic research, that data analysis is often slowed down or completely paralysed at the level of transcription because the tapes are not audible. Remarkably, research equipment is rarely discussed in oral literature fieldwork preparations. A good interview can be ruined by a low quality or faulty recording equipment. In the same way, a cunning researcher can mesmerize people with sophisticated digital equipment with nothing to show for it in terms of quality information recorded. Michael Patton in calling for modesty in the selection of research equipment observes that, "As a good hammer is essential to fine carpentry, a good tape recorder is indispensable to fine fieldwork" (380). Taking cue from Patton's observation, it is advisable to assemble the best tools for a given task.

This, however, does not mean going for the latest recording gadget in the market. It does not either imply using a digital recorder when one is challenged in computer knowledge. In selecting the tool to use in fieldwork, Finnegan advices that a fieldworker pays attention to convenience, portability, training needs, flexibility, security, compatibility, reliability, capacity and quality (Finnegan 1992, 65). In addition to Finnegan's prescription, I stress that a fieldworker understands the magnitude of the task before deciding on the tools required. The machines, even the best ones, come with their costs to the user, as Bruce Jackson confesses, 'every machine limits your mobility and defines your options' (109). Jackson advices field workers to know what their needs really are and desist from using more technology than is necessary. Equipment management takes time, attention and organization from other things and imposes constraints on where and when and with whom you carry out your research. The more complex and expensive the equipment, the more it can distract through the law of 'inverse attention'. In addition, trusting on mechanical recording can make a researcher ignore other forms of observation and documentation on the assumption that the machine is recording everything. One may even forget that machines often malfunction. A fieldworker is in what Americans call "Catch-22". If you fail to monitor the recording machine closely, the performance may proceed while the machine stopped long ago. If you constantly monitor the operations of the machine, you get distracted from observing the human interactions since a lot of action goes on that the tape cannot capture.

Data collection can be so engaging that within a few days, a fieldworker realises that so much data has been accumulated. The quantitative evidence for data collection will be in the cassettes or discs used for recording. To make the storage and retrieval of information systematic and easy to use, the researcher should be aware of the labelling protocol at the beginning of data collection. It is important that you number your recordings as you take them off the machine so as not to confuse them. Later you can write other necessary information on the cassette or disc such as:

- Title of the project:
- The name of the respondent:
- Name of the interviewer:
- Date and location of the recording:
- Subject recorded (for example, myths, life history):

It is not enough to label the cassette; the label may fall off with time. It is therefore recommended that a fieldworker records the details on each cassette or disc by announcing the details at the beginning of the recording as indicated in the interviewing process.

Performance Settings

Kenneth Goldstein identifies three scenarios of collecting narratives and observing performances as: artificial; natural and induced-natural settings (67-9). Artificial setting refers to a performance that is organized out of context to meet the needs of the collector. In a number of cases, researchers find that they have a lot to do within a very short time. If they have to wait to be assimilated in the community to get authentic texts, it may take forever. They resort to initiatives that bring artists and community members together at short notice to perform or provide information that meets research requirements. This is a common strategy in research. The second category is the natural setting in which fieldworkers take time to fit in the society, submerge their identities and wait for the performances to spring up when they must. In the natural setting, the researcher does not influence the performance in any way. He or she remains inconspicuous throughout the performance. The fieldworker, using participant observer approach then proceeds to observe and record the performances without attracting unnecessary attention. Any fieldworker yearns for this kind of fieldwork setting; nevertheless, it requires a lot of time, proficiency in the language of the performance and frequent trips to the field that may be too demanding on the researcher. University students, for example, operate within a tight semester programme and have only a few days to 'get a taste of the field'. Consequently, it is not possible to anticipate a natural setting where they can record authentic texts. In any case, even if they chance to get a natural setting for a performance, the number of students and their appearance in a new environment encourages artists to 'put up a show for visitors' which may be an exaggeration of the actual text. Artificial and natural settings are two extreme scenarios in a normal fieldwork situation. Despite its excellent opportunity, the natural setting that offers a fieldworker opportunity to observe a performance process in its purity, is not easy to come by as often as the researcher would wish and in addition, it does not yield as many texts as one would wish within a given timeframe.

University of Nairobi students conducting oral literature research in Maralal, Samburu District in November 2004 using induced natural setting *(Picture by Peter Wasamba)*

'Natural' setting in Goldstein's sense, however, is relatively unusual for the making of deliberate recordings. Not only are people's activities likely to be affected to some extent or another by the presence of a fieldworker but this presence may be especially intrusive if the researcher is, as often, trying to get a systematic recording of some event. Conducting research in a natural setting can persuade the fieldworker to abuse the host's hospitality by innocently engaging in clandestine research without informed consent. Goldstein's second category is a form of 'simulation': the re-enactment of a no longer current practice or the performance of 'an activity out of context for the purpose of an ethnographic description (Ellen, 72). Induced natural setting has advantages over 'natural setting' because it may not be possible to conduct fieldwork effectively in a purely natural context. "Merely waiting around hopefully may mean never having access to certain genres or events. It would be naïve to pretend that 'induced natural setting' may not yield quality information because we put up special performances for visitors or to celebrate special occasions. Compared to 'artificial' settings, induced performances may be closer to the normal interactions (Finnegan, 77). Goldstein's categorization, though helpful, is quite rigid. It assumes that a researcher cannot encounter the three settings within one community in one day. Experience indicates that depending on the audience available, the rapport creation process and demeanour of the fieldworker, these categories can change instantly. Therefore one is compelled to employ a hybrid setting which involves arranging for some 'simulated natural setting' to get enough texts.

Importance of Methodology

Research methodology has many dimensions and research methods do constitute only a small part of it. Having discussed what research methodology entails, and what research methods are, you may have noticed that the scope of research methodology is wider than that of research methods. Thus, when we talk of research methodology we not only talk of research methods but also consider the logic behind the methods we use in the context of our fieldwork project. We also explain why we are using a particular method or technique and why we are not using others so that research results are capable of being evaluated.

Research methodology is not fixed. It is realised in two contexts. We have research mythology as developed during the preparatory phase. It is speculative, theoretically grounded and ethologically sound but untested by the field. It is the design that governs a field study in the initial stages of data collection. It is always advisable to expect the field to modify theoretically designed methodology. This creates a slight difference between research methodology as designed and research methodology as implemented in the field. Regardless of the beautiful patterns we make, the sequences we plan to follow in the field and how predictable everything looks like, fieldwork defies research methodology designed in offices and lecture halls. The methodology emerges during the study and not before. It responds to the fecundity of life bubbling in the breasts and brains of those who create and consume verbal art and not the theoretical manoeuvres by arm-chair critics detached from the performance context.

A methodology worthy of the name will be continuously and reflexively developed as the study proceeds. Why interview? Why carry out a questionnaire survey? Why interview 25 rather than 500 informants? Decisions such as these are apparently often practical, but they carry very deeply entrenched and often unarticulated positions and consequences. They are often based on values and assumptions which influence the study, and as such therefore need to be fully interrogated in order to clarify the research decisions which are made. In this regard, it is important to monitor the extent of deviation of research methodology as actualized in the field from research methodology as conceived at the planning stages of the study.

Documentation, Preservation and Access

Every old man that dies is a library that burns

(Perks and Thomson ix: quoting Amadou Hampate Ba)

This chapter addresses post-data analysis phase in research. It explores options for bridging the missing link between ethnographic field research and archiving by interrogating the place of archiving in the entire fieldwork process, and the roles played by communities, researchers and archivists to promote access in the digital dispensation. Research is an academic enterprise. It is not an end in itself. It is a risky intellectual investment geared towards knowledge generation with an ultimate goal of making life better for humankind and the environment. Post-data analysis phase is critical as it ensures that the yields of research in terms of innovations and discoveries are funnelled into the hub of preservation for increased utilization. We commence the discussion with a reflection on the link between data processing, analysis and preservation, then we proceed to what archiving is in oral literature studies and the challenges that exist. Thereafter, we examine the key challenges to preservation. The chapter concludes with emphasis on fostering closer collaboration between all research stakeholders in preservation and dissemination of the intangible heritage using both traditional and digital media.

Fieldworkers are keen to capture the voice and atmosphere that condition performances for ease of analysis and interpretation. It should be noted that data collection and processing are meant to make significant contributions to knowledge while at the same time benefitting the researcher(s) in getting academic qualifications, monetary rewards, or meeting the contractual research obligations to clients. This raises the question of, what happens after data analysis and report writing. This question exposes a fissure in the research process that has not received requisite attention from orature fieldworkers in the recent past. This disconnect is what I refer to as the missing link between ethnographic fieldwork and archiving. Oral literature in Africa is a fighting genre, partly because practitioners who directly live on verbal art, experience and perform it are mostly locals who get familiar with it, and with time take it for granted. Researchers too do not give equal consideration to the preservation of the research data as they do to data collection and analysis. They hardly pay serious attention to the documentation and preservation of oral texts for wider access.

The initial attempts to preserve oral performances focused on writing, storage in audio and audio-visual forms, internet and human memory. This was followed by converting live performances into written texts which were then translated into languages widely used in the world for education and cultural exchange. Scholars debating the resilience of oral literature are alarmed by this trend. Performances which, not long ago, were rendered live before physically present and enthusiastic audiences, are increasingly being reduced to writing or digital files that can be enjoyed by individuals in private places. This phenomenon has elicited various reactions with some arguing that employing writing to oral performances extends their use while others mourn the death of the hitherto vibrant genre under the spear of the pen.

Advocates of written oral performances reason that writing though complementary allows for documentation and preservation of performances which ensures that verbal creations are not lost or forgotten. Among other benefits, written oral literature assists in studying the culture of a given community; enables storage, reproduction and sharing of the performed texts beyond their original boundaries. Scholars of oral literature also contend that written texts promote access, prevent loss of the text and make analysis possible. Taban lo Liyong (1972) in encouraging storage of performances in written form argues that "since most of our vital knowledge is still retained in the memory, having been deposited there through the spoken word, the best way for us to get native intellectual nourishment is through bringing this knowledge into circulation, giving the oral knowledge a competitive place in the educational programme; putting it down in a form which preserves it" (71). Writing allows critics to study a given text several times moving back and forth with much ease while noting their comments down where necessary without missing any segment of the performance. Further, printed form makes it easier for a large group of people to be exposed to oral literature texts from other places cheaply and readily thereby helping to spur people's interest which ensures the growth of the discipline. It is also important to remember that there is a thin line between written and performed oral literature texts because some of the oral performances are just recitations of the written texts.

In spite of the stated advantages of reducing oral performances into written texts, we are apprehensive that this trend, if encouraged, may herald the demise of the genre that for centuries has remained the hallmark of genuine African creativity, entertainment, education and cultural vitality. We note that experiencing an oral text in written form kills the element of performance, excludes audience participation and suggests genre immobility which is alien to oral literature. Oral texts are ever changing depending on various circumstances and therefore the written version may not be able to capture the changes. Oral literature by definition is a special performance that is living. It is too fluid to be frozen into a static written document. Consequently, a printed form of performance is only a partial picture of the total text. The artist adds non-verbal elements in the performance which are lost in the printed form. It is these non-verbal elements which carry a deeper and fuller meaning of the texts. Performance also allows for verbal variability and dynamism which makes it easier to interpret the intent of a text that is orally performed than the one which is written down. Alternative interpretations of a written performance from other cultures may turn out to be wrong. Writing also leads to the death of oral artists because the written text is so impersonal, and in many cases is authored by a researcher. Reduction of live performances into printed books is therefore not a viable approach to the preservation of oral literature.

Performance and Memory

One area that is yet to be addressed exhaustively is the symbiotic relationship between field research and the preservation of oral literature in Africa. There is need to reflect on the strategies that have been used in the past to preserve oral literature to assess their appropriateness and sustainability (Wasamba 2005, 2). While it is incontestable that oral literature can be preserved through recordings in print and electronic media for storage and wider dissemination, it is our contention that oral literature can survive best in its original form – as performance. It is only "performance that makes tradition perceptible and it is also the source of ensuing text" (Vansina, J: 36). In early 2003 while conducting research in Matuga Division of Kwale District, in the Coastal strip of Kenya, I encountered a unique group of oral artists who were very ready to perform but could not do so because of what I discovered to be an acute memory lapse.

Through empathy, I could see the frustrations on the faces of women and men who were excited that finally their worth to the society had been recognized by an important person from the university, yet so sad that they could not perform the narratives they had been good at not long ago. Such artists requested for more time to put together fragments of the narratives they could salvage from remote memory. They had to transport themselves back to those gone years in order to remember the texts well. I encouraged them to perform the segments they could remember without feeling ashamed. This process was painfully slow, but very rewarding in the end. The artists started recreating the texts through a series of rehearsals. With each rehearsal, their performances improved. The fact that they could remember and perform their stories challenged other members of the audience to participate in the telling of the same stories or introducing new ones for novelty. The number of artists volunteering to perform increased with every performance. By the end of my visit, the artists had seen the need to perform on a regular basis to celebrate their oral heritage.

Where the story telling was slow to start, a helping method was used to ask for stories by theme: 'Do you know a story about a proud person who is punished by *jinnis* (spirits)? The strategy worked so well because as Kidane (2002) argues, "once the first story is told, some element of that story triggers another story and can lead on to as many as four or five tales" (9). My observation in early 2003 was later corroborated by the report of Susan Mukabi Muriba, my student, who collected songs among the Kikuyu in late 2003. The student identified memory loss as a major challenge to the performance and preservation of oral literature. This is what she reported about Kagema, the famous oral artist among the Kikuyu of Central Kenya:

> The old man was very receptive and easy to probe. Being a man of eighty years, his memory was fading and he admitted that he could not remember so many things because of advancing age. For example, he did not know when the song was sung, who sang it first, where and in which season. He tried to sing other songs but

sang only one line and admitted that he had forgotten the rest. For example, he started a very interesting song known as *kibaata* but sang only one verse which he kept on repeating before he finally admitted that he could not get the rest. He also begun a circumcision song that was sung by *ihii* (the uncircumcised), but failed to remember a whole verse. (Wasamba, P 2005: 5)

These observations suggest that when proverbs, stories and poems are not performed regularly, they are stored in the inner chamber of the artist's memory. The texts stay in the memory for a given time before they are forgotten completely. I also realized that when artists are not made to feel valued, they go for other activities that ensure their self-esteem and survival. It is therefore urgent that oral heritage be revived and performed in their most natural form in order to be preserved. Those who glorify preservation through performance are normally stunned when confronted with the question: What happens to the texts after a connoisseur dies?

Archiving Oral Texts

In their introduction to *The Oral History Reader* 2nd Edition (2009), Perks Robert and Alistar Thomson quoting the famous African proverb attributed to Amadou Hampate Ba reiterates that, "Every old man that dies is a library that burns" (ix). The proverb underlies both the importance and urgency of documenting and archiving oral texts for continuity and expanded utilization. Archiving refers to preservation and promotion of access to a collection of literature over time, without regard for how frequently these materials are being read or used (Guthrie, 58). It is a futuristic project that entails thinking well ahead, to a time maybe decades or centuries in the future, by which time the names of individual informants are no longer of any importance from a data protection point of view (Zeitlyn, 1–2).

Archives have traditionally been established in conjugation with scientific studies. The purpose of a research archive is to collect, store and promote continued use of data and metadata. Researchers are usually conversant with data but not all understand metadata. The metadata is data that explains data. It is data that provides additional contextually rich information about the condensed data in public circulation. For example, we are not likely to include all the detailed information we collect in the field like who we interviewed, when, where, with who and the methods used to compile, analyze and interpret data. The raw information from which we sieve data is what metadata is. Data without metadata is too sketchy for any meaningful analysis. Kuula correctly observes that the documentation is critical for the re-usage of metadata: "Regardless of the data format, proper documentation is crucial because the data may be used many years after its collection and very likely for purposes that are different from the original. Metadata is necessary for the re-user of the data to indicate the intellectual content, geographical and temporal coverage, and the methods employed in its collection. Only well-documented data can be re-used" (3).

As emphasized by Kuula, the way in which research is conducted and documented determines not only the archival value of the text but also its usability in future. This explains why researchers have a stake in how archiving is done.

Interest in studying folk traditions and maintaining them dates back to the Egyptian modern Renaissance in the 19th and early 20th Centuries. Interest in folklore then, was not driven by rescue ethnography which characterized folklore scholarship in the 20th Century, but a demonstrated commitment by scholars to appreciate the role of folklore in shaping national culture. Traditional archiving was then orally based and entirely dependent on memory. "An observer reported his/her experience orally, casting it in an initial message. A second party heard it and passed it on. From party to party it was passed on until the last party acting as informant told it to the recorder" (Vansina 29).

Even though the threat to verbal culture due to rapid modernization has dominated academic discussions in conferences and symposia, the primary challenge for oral literature in the 21st Century is that of preservation for access, and not fear of its death. Archiving of oral literature texts, in particular, is unique. It contributes to democratization of experiences by giving voices to common men and women hardly considered important in mainstream discourse. Where attempts have been made in the past to record and preserve personal histories, there is almost always only one perspective – that of the authorities, politicians, business icons and academics. Common women and men, the youth, the elderly and persons with disability are never given space to voice themselves into reality. If at all they get space, it is in a court of law or in other uninspiring situations.

It is rare to find archives where the common men and women get a pedestal to celebrate their struggles and share their low points in their own voices and their own terms. In cases where oral literature interviews have been conducted, documentation and archiving for expanded exploitation have been wanting. While the interview recordings are considered a central historical artefact that provides a level of emotion and humanity not available in text transcripts, often "these recordings sit unused after a written transcript is produced" (Klemmer, S.R: 90). Fieldworkers, librarians and archivists, especially in the developing world, have not been able to find the means to make recordings searchable by users geographically removed from them. In addition, they have not been able to disseminate their collections to new audiences, "a process that is still frequently hampered, not only by inadequate resources and entrenched attitudes but also by poor documentation and absence of legal consent" (Perks & Thomson 334).

Disconnect between Researchers and Archivists

Ellen Swain, commenting on the lack of collaboration between oral historians, librarians and archivists over the past fifty years wonders aloud:

> Why aren't archivists and librarians, early leaders in the profession, more prominent and visible in oral history circles today? Why hasn't the role of oral history in the library been a topic of discussion in recent scholarship? (355)

Swain, in her survey, notes that there is lack of collaboration and harmony in the way researchers and archivists operate. She further observes that some collectors have been rather cavalier in preserving, documenting and depositing their data. And some information professionals, whilst recognizing the potential that oral history has for … 'filling the gaps' in collections, or for providing researchers with 'road maps', have voiced concerns about their roles (333-4). The problematic relationship Swain identifies above is represented by the two antagonistic camps led by Clive Cochrane and Bruce Bruemmer. Cochrane blames fieldworkers for fissure while Bruemmer faults archivists. By 1985, Cochrane insisted that field workers had concentrated too much on recording practices and not enough on access. Six years later, Bruemmer argued that archivists by not exploiting the full potential of digital technology 'are at fault for the lack of access to oral history collections' (Swain, 352). Kirk and Miller avoid the blame game that consumes Cochrane and Bruemmern. They fault the archiving lacuna on methodological deficiencies, especially lack of archiving framework for fieldworkers. In their assessment, the missing link is "the framework to enable fieldworkers to make others see what they saw in the field from recording the performances to analysis and archiving" (Kirk and Miller, 1986: 21).

The divided opinion on the role of collectors and archivists in the preservation and dissemination of recorded texts is indicative of the disciplinary divide between archivists and researchers. In my research experience for over a decade, I have gathered that there is very limited structured engagement between collectors and archivists in Kenya. Corti (2000) explains the gap on conflicting theoretical approaches to research and archiving, academic backgrounds and attendant attitude problems and the work environment. In his opinion, attitudes to archiving in the humanities and social sciences are often rather negative:

> Researchers are most concerned about confidentiality and any agreements that may have been made between the collector and the informant at the time of collection. They may also be uncertain about the quality of their data, and afraid that subsequent users will find fault with the data collection and/or analysis. Researchers who have personally worked in the field also feel it is impossible to share the experience of 'being there'; secondary users cannot be aware of all the details and backgrounds to the collection of the material. (9–10.)

The attitude to archives adopted by fieldworkers referred to by Corti is problematic. While they readily use existing archive materials as an aid to both teaching and research, they are not greatly in favour of archiving their own materials. In my opinion, this is not deliberate. It is based on the notion that collection and archiving are independent and exclusive practices that should not be considered together. Further, this school has always argued that researchers do not have to bother about archiving since it is not their profession. Archivists too, argue that they do not have to know about how the data they receive and look after was collected, let alone participate in collection. This standoff hurts preservation of oral literature material. It calls for a rapprochement for a symbiotic relationship between field research and the preservation of verbal arts in Africa.

Stuart Davies contends that, oral heritage 'occupies an ambivalent, uncomfortable and vulnerable position in museums' (Davies, S 74). It is like an illegitimate member of the family. The Kenyan situation, where the National Archives of Kenya (NAK) suspended receiving voice-recorded texts in 1982, confirms Davies' concern. In an interview with M'reria (2009), the Acting Manager of the National Archives of Kenya (NAK), archiving of recorded interviews and performances were officially suspended by the government in 1982. Before this time, the recorded oral texts were kept at NAK. The section was, however, weak and lacking in expertise and valuable collections. NAK scrapped the oral history section in 1982 on expert advice from UNESCO. The expert argued that there was too much duplication in the collection of folklore by various government agencies such as the Institute of African Studies (IAS) at the University of Nairobi, the British East African Institute (BEAI), NAK, and the Voice of Kenya (VoK).

The irony of it is that after the UNESCO report, all the agencies involved quietly suspended systematic collection, analysis, documentation, archiving and utilization of folklore. "Other agencies involved in folklore collection are not guided by any policy and are lacking in coordination which has ensured duplication and lack of access to the collected material due to poor archiving standards employed, if any" (M'reria, Interview July 27 2009). M'reria's observations are corroborated by the government policy document on intangible heritage that does not make it obligatory for researchers to hand over material to the archives. The position taken by NAK is not strange. Voices of tradition in the archiving world have argued that "the function of museums is to preserve and interpret artefacts and that oral heritage is technically difficult to include in a gallery space, and that it is an expensive luxury" (Perks and Thomson, 337). In the absence of the NAK, the institutions that have tried in modest ways to collect and preserve oral texts are the universities and research institutions, but without adequate funding and proper regulation on archiving procedures.

University of Nairobi and Archiving of Oral Text

For more than thirty years, oral literature students under the supervision of their lecturers, and the support from the University of Nairobi, have served as primary archivists for the oral literature collections. The students have been able to record, process and deliver the products to the lecturers in charge of oral literature fieldwork. The first class text to be used by university students in Kenya was a product of fieldwork conducted in 1969 by oral literature students under the guidance of Taban Lo Liyong. The product of this fieldwork, *Popular Cultures of East Africa* (1971), provided one of the early textbooks to be used in teaching oral literature in universities in Kenya.

Researchers have often explained their reluctance to record performances with archiving in mind on lack of archiving skills. This fear is reinforced by Baron and Spitzer who contend that making folk traditions accessible to wider audiences demands "mastery, within folkloristic frameworks of physical settings and techniques of presentations and technologies of lighting, sound reinforcement, film and audio production, design and stage management, as well as in scholarly understanding" (Baron and

Spitzer ix). This is not necessarily the case since archiving-conscious data collection may not require expertise that the fieldworker may not have like hiring sound engineers, professional photographers, archivists, librarians and IT experts. Archiving only requires a field worker to recognize these as areas he or she needs to work with. The proposed approach embraces the spirit of interdisciplinary engagement. In the Kenyan situation, it calls for collaboration between producers of information, researchers, preservers, disseminators and the end-users. The players may include but are not limited to research units such as Departments of Literature, Sociology, History, Institute of African Studies and end users like Media Owners Association, National archives and National Museums of Kenya.

The notion that researchers are not specialized in archiving and therefore should not involve themselves in the work of librarians and archivists is misleading because poor archiving systems in place hurt researchers more than the archivists. Fieldworkers have the task of collecting, recording and studying materials of folklore in order to make them accessible to artists, scholars, writers and civil society. Raphael Samuel, a pioneering historian, argued as early as 1971 that the role of the collector of the spoken word is that of an archivist. Like a historian, he or she retrieves and stores priceless information which would otherwise be lost. His or her greatest contribution is in the collecting and safe preservation of the material rather than in the use he can immediately find for it (19 – 22).

Guthrie adds the missing link in Samuel's argument by asserting that the purpose of archiving is to increase access. The "development of the existing archiving system was not predicated primarily on a desire to archive; rather, archiving has been essentially a bi-product of the need to provide access" (58). Involvement of researchers in matters of archiving is no longer an option; it is demanded by the digitized information society we operate in. Researchers should work closely with archivists for the very reason that the products of their intellectual investments are directly affected by the way their collections are preserved and disseminated. This is not to forget that, many researchers waste time and money looking for material that is already available but not accessible. I'm more than convinced that the predicament we are in now is because of the way researchers and archivists have operated solo and in competition with each other in the past. None of the parties can succeed in their redefined mandates alone. The time to compliment each other's effort is now. An oral heritage researcher is not in competition with an archivist. At best he or she is a: "collaborator, critic, colleague, teacher, and friend" (Grele 15).

Archivists and Neutrality

Archivists, like fieldworkers, have also been reluctant to develop interest in what researchers do. They have defended this aloofness on the notion of neutrality. One of the strongest deterrents to oral history's acceptance among archivists and special collection librarians has been the idea that they, "as neutral, impartial curators of collections, can or should not 'create' records" (Swain 346). Consequently, traditional archivists have been reluctant to privilege any particular approach to meaning or inquiry, much less to incorporate it in their taxonomies. Kolovos, a strong advocate of neutrality in archiving, is quoted by Frisch as a defender of the status quo:

> As an archivist it's not my job to create new meaning, it is just to try to stabilize the meaning of a recording or document in relation to the larger grouping from which it comes – to maintain it as best as possible within the intellectual context of its creation and use. Making new meaning is the job of a researcher using materials. (Frisch 107)

Derek Reimer in an attempt to correct this notion argues that archivists are the best collectors. He urges fellow archivists to consider themselves "historical researchers" or "cultural conservators" without losing the opportunity of recording vanishing resources because of some arbitrary linear subdivision of the world of knowledge which says that archivists do not participate in the creation of records. In his opinion, archivists are the most knowledgeable about collection deficiencies and can best fill in the gaps (Swain 346). Archivists cannot detach themselves from data collection citing objectivity because "personhood cannot be left behind, cannot be left out of the research process" (Frankfort-Nachmias, Chava and David Nachmias, 75). Torn Nesmith, a supporter of collaboration between researchers and archivists, focuses on postmodern theory to illuminate the collaborative role of archivists in mediating and thus shaping the knowledge available in archives:

> Postmodernism shatters the notion that archivists are or can be objective caretakers of documents as their bias, interests, and backgrounds shape the ways in which they collect and maintain archival holdings. Nesmith asserts that archivists 'help author

> records by the very act of determining what authoring them means
> and involves, or what the provenance of the record is. (Nesmith 24)

From the foregoing polemics, it is apparent that archivists must assume an active role in oral arts discourse; collaborate with each other and colleagues in other fields, and to be attuned to current scholarship needs if archives and special collection departments are to be viable and market-oriented research sources in the future. Wennstedt summarizes the connection between data collection and archiving with the phrase "collect, preserve and scientifically treat and publish material concerning our immaterial cultural heritage" (123). The tasks outlined by Wennstedt cannot be accomplished by fieldworkers alone or archivists on their own. It requires a combined effort strongly backed by digital technology.

Digital Technology and Archiving

Digitizing is the process by which material with the artist, respondent, researcher or already in an archive such as tapes, photographs and transliterations, is converted to a computer-readable form. Initially, the entry of African oral literature into the web through digitization sounded like a myth. The Internet was then considered undeniably a product of a literate, westernized technologically advanced society. It did not take long for cultural researchers to discover that in its functions and developing culture, the Web is an oral medium with many oral characteristics such as temporal immediacy, the use of formulaic devices, and presence of extra textual content, development of community and the use of hypertext (Wasamba 2007, 114).

Nicholas Negroponte in the last few pages of his book, *Epilogue: An Age of Optimism*, points out candidly that "being digital" is an unstoppable force, one destined to triumph because of its specific powers of decentralizing, globalizing, harmonizing, and empowering (229).

Now that it has been confirmed that the web is not a threat to cultural research, documentation, preservation and dissemination, the apocalyptic words of Richard McLuham, the internet and cultural enthusiast, has come true. McLuham, a futurist, argues that we look at the present through a rear-view mirror and that in our advancement, 'we march backwards into the future,' (McLuham R, 26). The deduction one makes from McLuham's prophesy is that technology does not kill or replace the old, instead, the old forces modern technology to serve its traditional needs. Digitization therefore makes it possible to bridge the gap between data collection, preservation and access. It brings fieldworkers, archivists and users together in a complementary partnership. In his concluding contribution to the review of "Critical Developments," Michael Frisch writing from the cusp of the digital frontier supports McLuham's position and, as if to echo Walter Ong (1982) on primary and secondary orality, asserts that digitalization has the potential to "return aurality to oral history" (Frisch 113).

Ong and Secondary Orality

Ong contends oral texts composed and performed by 'traditional' communities are old and new at the same time due to their adaptive nature which encourages hybridization between the old and the new. What each generation inherits in terms of oral narratives, songs, proverbs and riddles is not what it passes on. Each generation modifies oral texts based on the pertinent issues of the day, quality of oral artists, nature of audience and technological support available. This incremental development of texts is the core of 'tradition' as opposed to antiquity. While new communications technologies appear to contract world diversity and portend the loss of intimacy with their speed and sometimes impersonal qualities, there are also those cultural groups resisting gentrification by purposefully using the very technologies, economies, and information that overwhelm others to enforce cultural continuity. In the end our concern must be human agency first at the community level to advocate for appropriate culture continuity as a fundamental freedom and means to better quality of life (Baron and Spitzer xvii).

The value digital technology adds to the redefined relationship between oral heritage researchers and archivists, is elucidated by: Bret Eynon (1999), Ellen Swain (2006), Tiina Mhalamaki (2000, 2001), Negroponte (1995) and Wasamba (2007) among others. Reflecting in a special *Oral History Review* issue on oral history at the millennium, Eynon argues that the spread of digital technology is 'forcing archives to rethink their roles, functions, and to confront difficult questions of security, protection and accessibility' (Eynon 1999, 42). Eynon suggests that in the new technological dispensation, archivists must step out of the box and engage oral historians by showing interest in their scholarship and interview tapes; providing leadership in access, legal, and preservation issues; promoting the importance of depositing oral histories in the archives; and making contacts to help develop archival holdings. Swain, echoing Bruce Bruemmer calls for a 'proactive advocacy' in which archivists construct relationships between the oral history and the library and archives not only by attending oral history conferences and meetings but also by inviting oral historians to participate in archival forums (Swain 356).

Tiina Mhalamaki (2001) goes beyond theorizing on the connection between field research and preservation by demonstrating how folklore field research can be navigated through the stages of data collection, cataloguing, archiving to the final destination which is online access. Relying on the research conducted at the University of Turku, Finland, she describes the progression of research material, mainly tape-recorded interviews from the field to the Sound Archive of Folklore and Comparative Religion of the TKU Archive. Based on the study, Mahlamäki (2001) in "Some guidelines for the archiving of qualitative research data in the digital era," points out that there are three main areas one should address in dealing with data collection and preservation for increased access (13). Louise Corti, concurs with Mahalamaki on the need to develop documentation standards that promote the use of digital materials for research and teaching requirements. He too encourages archives to take up the challenge without delay and supply researchers with information on the existence of qualitative data and its potential uses (Corti, 17).

Importance of Digitization

The reasons for digitization are varied and numerous. Digital technology addresses problems of data organization, exploitation and borderless access that have bothered researchers for years. Previously, the content of these collections was rarely organized; much less indexed in any depth, and the actual audio or video could not be searched or browsed in any useful way. As a result, "the considered potential of audio and video documents to support high impact, vivid, thematic, and analytic engagement with meaningful issues, personalities and contexts remained largely untapped" (Frisch, 102). Digitization, as suggested by Frisch, addresses gaps in verbal art's international dialogue. It has great advantages for archivists and researchers alike as it permits speedy, simple searching and copying of the materials (Kurkela 1999).

Contrary to the common perception, materials are not digitized merely to rescue them from loss or poor handling. New digital technologies are transforming the ways in which researchers and archivists record, preserve, catalogue, interpret, share and present data. On an Internet-backed platform, the use of the material is not dependent on time and place. Internet makes it faster and easier to use large amounts of research material because it can be handled, searched and studied using the archive database. It should also be remembered that unlike hard copies in archives, several researchers can access the data at the same time and from different locations (Saarinen, 119- 120.) What all of these approaches have in common is the promise of flexibility to the researcher, the user and archivists. From large scale archive to small community project, to home or family collections, it is going to be more and more flexible to hear, see, browse, search, study, refine, select, export, and make use of audio and video extracts from oral histories by directly engaging the documentation itself (Frisch 110).

Frisch concludes that we are witnessing the emergence of a 'post-documentary sensibility' which breaks down the distinction between the verbal text document source and the oral history documentary product, and suggests that 'new digital tools and the rich landscape of practice they define may become powerful resource in restoring one of the original appeals of oral history – to open new dimensions of understanding and engagement through the broadly inclusive sharing and interrogation of memory. The 'post-documentary sensibility' Frisch refers to is also realized at the level of audience. Conventionally, audience in oral performances is supposed to be physically present, have a sense of belonging and remain active. The modern society, characterized by displacement, individualism and mobility has made it expensive to assemble traditional audience.

Oral artists in Africa have been forced to 'chase' retreating audience in urban centres, schools, funerals and bars with varying levels of success. This explains why majority of oral artists in Africa belong to the most impoverished segment of the society. To bridge this gap, digital archiving creates a versatile audience that is virtual, accessible, more private, autonomous and social at the same time. Oral artists and other custodians of folk knowledge are removed from the oblivion of empty performances spaces in the villages due to education system and rural-urban migration to the global performance arena proffered by the cyberspace. Further, the electronic media eliminates the gap between an oral artist and audience, since either can become the other with baffling facility. In illustrating how the electronic media enhances the transactional enterprise between the artist and audience, George Landow argues that if the Homeric bard and his listeners are partners in the same experience, one might just as well identify the electronic reader with *the Homeric bard*. In a hypertext environment, *an oral artist* constructs meaning and narrative from fragments provided by someone else, "by another author or by many other authors" (Landow: 117). The principle of using some segments of an oral narrative or song to link up with other related narratives or songs is the logic behind hypertext in the Internet.

Challenges of Digitization

With all the accolades heaped on the promise of digital technology in bridging the gap between research and access to information, one may assume that it is a cure-it-all prescription for the shortcomings experienced in data collection, analysis, preservation and dissemination. The challenges already experienced and those anticipated confirm that this may not be the case. Some of the challenges researchers and archivists are likely to face include poor recording in analogue tapes, software challenges, poor infrastructure, low consumption capacity, technophobia, the North-South digital divide and lack of clear government policy. Digitization of oral texts initially recorded using traditional analogue technology can be quite daunting. From the economic perspective, the project may, at the face value, not look viable because the total cost of digitizing collections and maintaining the information will certainly exceed any revenue likely to be generated by making the materials accessible. Further, the information digitized must be continuously updated to keep pace with the technological developments in IT. Failure to do so can render the collection obsolete and inaccessible within a very short time. Migration from the old file formats into the new formats can be expensive and risky. This is because in information communication technology (ICT), nothing is constant. Since it is impossible to find a lasting software for archiving, the best that IT experts can do is to avoid "lock-up" when technology changes. In such a situation, access is stifled when migration to new technology is hindered by the enormous financial investment to overhaul the digital archiving platform. Looting and misuse are also other likely regrettable consequences of the promoting access to the intangible African cultural heritage, especially in the Internet.

Digitization is a slow process, and many solutions and decisions have to be made on techniques, formats, copyright and data protection. Collaboration between archives is of great importance. The major challenge that oral literature raises in the cyberspace is that of intellectual property rights. For instance, how can the digitized performances in the cyberspace be protected and legally exploited for the benefit of the oral artists? Who owns copyright to oral narratives, songs and epics posted in the cyberspace? In the developing countries where enforcement of copyright legislations is weak, artists are least likely to gain from their artistic labour (Wasamba 2007, 117).

It is interesting to note that the more we digitize our research and archiving practices, the more we are likely to realize the resilient value of traditional archiving. In Africa communities yet to be reached by power grids, computers and internet systems, conversion to digital archiving may sound as a pipe-dream. In such cases, traditional archiving practices will continue to thrive. Digital archiving will not therefore replace the traditional archiving system but augment it. When the two approaches are encouraged, information will be stored and disseminated to technology rich and technology poor societies equally without discrimination. It will also encourage collaboration between fieldworkers and archivists in a mutually beneficial manner without undue haste or artificial crisis. In justifying the place of digital storage, we also opined that paper documents decay, wear out with continuous handling and restrict access to a single storage location. Yet, backward as this old technology of preservation may look, it still promises the most reliable method of preservation because its format does not require any upgrading like various electronic programmes. It does not require computers, internet based communication or availability of reliable power supply.

We root for a fieldwork design that integrates archiving into data collection and processing procedures to address the gap between data collection and archiving. It is important that researchers acquaint themselves with traditional and contemporary archiving practices in order to ensure that preservation component is inbuilt in the fieldwork from its inception in terms of the research design; transcription protocols; translation protocols, data analysis procedures and archiving protocols. Most important of all, researchers should infuse internationally acceptable ethical standards into the data collection and analysis processes such as informed consent and confirmation before publication to make the material useful to archivists. When this is done, fieldworkers will succeed in going beyond collection to preservation and use. Archivists will also reclaim their original passion which was in knowing how the material they stored and offered to the public was collected. Digital technology offers a platform for collaboration and enhanced partnership between these two key players.

Data Analysis

My research partners usually confess that fieldwork in oral literature is a memorable period of adventure and learning. A corpus of information in the form of interview transcripts, documented performances, photos, video clips, field notes and journals is carefully harvested using customized research instruments such as voice recorders, cameras, notebooks and memory. The major challenge is encountered once the actual data collection is done and the second stage of data processing, analysis, and interpretation commences. Researchers, especially beginners, suddenly become alive to the puzzle of how to draw valid meaning from qualitative data.

Most important is the challenge of identifying and using methods of analysis that are practical, communicable, and consistent with the genre. This fear is not reserved for young researchers alone. A number of career researchers find themselves overwhelmed with the information they collect from the field in terms of data processing, analysis and interpretation. This explains, in part, why offices of collectors are stacked with dusty tapes which are not transcribed, yellow transcripts which are not analyzed and other forms of deteriorating data in need of processing and analysis. The gap between data collection and analysis has necessitated a shift in fieldwork methodology with researchers increasingly debating on a host of new questions as they design, conduct, and report on their research. This problem is not brought about by the inability of disciplines in humanities to use qualitative data analysis methods. The problem is caused by lack of clarity in frameworks to be employed in data analysis and interpretation, especially in disciplines that border humanities and social sciences like oral literature.

The other impediment to data analysis is the assumption that qualitative data analysis is a preserve of social scientists. It is made to look technical and a reserve for scholars with quantitative research methods background only. This chapter addresses data analysis in Oral Literature, by considering data collection and processing as part of an analytical process. We commence discussion by reflecting on the place of oral literature criticism in Africa and the meaning of data analysis. This is followed by an explication of data transcription and translation processes. Before concluding the chapter, we introduce Computer Assisted Qualitative Data Analysis (CAQDA) in oral literature and discuss the prospects and limitations of the ICT in aiding researchers to organize, interpret and preserve data.

Oral Literature Criticism

Literature on the analysis and interpretation of verbal arts in Kenya indicates an inadequate engagement with both the raw data collected from the field and secondary data already published. There are a number of publications on the oral literatures of various communities, but most of them stop at the documentation of the performances and a cursory introduction of the book in question. Data analysis in oral literature is still struggling to establish a hybrid tradition that harmonizes the literary, linguistic and social science analytic traditions emblematic of the genre's heredity. In this scenario, one is persuaded to agree with Jan Janheinz's (1968) declaration that "Oral literature (in Africa) has not been subjected to literary analysis" (23. *parenthesis mine*). Although a lot has happened since the scholar raised the red flag, a lot still needs to be done to address the analytical lacuna.

Proper analysis of primary data can only be meaningful when data collection is methodologically informed and theoretically grounded. The two topics have been addressed extensively in the previous chapters. In a number of published researches in oral literature, it is rare to find systematic documentation of how data was collected, organized and analyzed. Not that this information does not exist at all, nor is it because researchers are not thorough in their research activities. The missing link has been the framework to enable oral literature researchers make 'others see what they see in the data' (Kirk and Miller, 21). It is a common practice among fieldworkers to transcribe, translate and publish in book form what they submit as the oral literature of community X. What is presented in these books is what a fieldworker believes to be the product of the research. Without sounding cynical, it would be naïve to accept a product of research in total absence of the process that led to it. Fieldworkers ought to realize that not everybody is observing what they are doing in the field. They should not be too economical with the processes that take place before, during and after data collection. Inadequate information does not only impede data analysis, it often leads to doubts about data integrity and claims made based on the study. Vansina is correct in pointing out that data collection must take on board the methods to be applied in data analysis since, "Only when it is clear how the text stands to the performance and the latter to the tradition can an analysis of the contents of the message begin" (33). As if to echo Vansina, Lynn Abrams asserts that the process of interviewing cannot be disaggregated from the expected outcome (3). Vansina and Abrams suggest that data analysis is embedded in the research methodology.

The gap between data collection and analysis is currently attracting the attention of oral literature researchers. Fieldworkers are increasingly debating on a host of questions as they plan, conduct, and report on their research. Some of the questions asked in methodology forums touch on the state of criticism of African oral literature; when data analysis begins; data integrity through transcription and translation processes; how to make sense of the data; how to arrive at interpretations; and how best to preserve the research data for future use. Methodologists in oral literature emphasize a chain-link that binds conceptualization of the research problem to data collection, processing, analysis, interpretation, preservation and dissemination. Knowing what you are looking for (*research question*) before the commencement of the study inevitably aids you to think about the 'how and why' (*methodology*) of getting that information and how you assemble (*processing*) the information dictates how you will analyze data (*analysis*) to confirm whether you have found what you were looking for (*interpretation*) before you expose it to wider consumption (*dissemination*) for improved access beyond immediate needs (*archiving*). Put simply, a researcher should know what he or she is looking for; how to assemble data that might have answers to the question; how to get the relevant information from the data so assembled; how to share the findings with stakeholders and how to preserve the material for increased access. As Walcott puts it, there is merit in open mindedness and willingness to enter a research setting looking for questions as well as answers, but it is "impossible to embark upon research without some idea of what one is looking for and foolish not to make that quest explicit"(157).

Analysis is not an invention of scholars. We conduct analysis every day, every time, outside academics. For example, when looking for life time partners, we sample, cluster, evaluate, and compare who we prefer based on our original expectations. Data analysis is a scholarly extension of the discrimination, clustering and interpretation that we continuously do in order to facilitate growth in knowledge. According to Edward Tufte, our existence is unavoidably analytical otherwise we would not survive in this information-thick world. He explains that we survive because of our marvellous and everyday capacities to:

....select, edit, single out, structure, highlight, group, pair, merge, harmonize, synthesize, focus, organize, condense, reduce, boil down, choose, categorize, catalogue, classify, refine, abstract, scan, look into, idealize, isolate, discriminate, distinguish, screen, sort, pick over, group, pigeonhole, integrate, blend, average, filter, lump, skip, smooth, chunk, inspect, approximate, cluster, aggregate, outline, summarize, itemize, review, dip into, flip through, browse, glance into, leaf through, skim, list, glean, synopsize, winnow wheat from chaff, and separate the sheep from the goats.(50)

The rich vocabulary Tufte assembles to describe what analysis entails and why it is unavoidable in life provides enough justification for its application to research, which is a refined academic activity.

Data analysis in oral literature research entails generating data by recording performances and conducting in-depth interviews. This is followed by transcribing and translating audio/audio-visual recordings; checking transcripts for accuracy and clarity and analysing and interpreting data before presenting findings in a report. Data analysis in qualitative research is thus an ongoing process that begins with the commencement of data collection and cannot therefore be suspended to the end-tail of research. It starts with fieldwork and journeys with it diligently, through all the stages until the final report is done.

Transcription and Translation

No meaningful data analysis can take place without a deliberate effort to ensure data hygiene through transcription and translation. Transcription is a lengthy and tedious process of actualizing into writing the sound data embedded in electronic media such as tapes or discs. It takes averagely four hours of intense engagement to transcribe both sides of one audio-tape of 30 minutes length, if clarity is optimal. The exercise is energy sapping that at the end of it all, the neck is paining, eyes are fuzzy, shoulders aching and concentration is at the lowest. Consequently, there is a tendency among researchers to give attention to fieldwork and data analysis without assessing how transcription and translation are handled. It is important to remember that the production and use of transcripts are critical research activities that should not be approached merely as formalities that prepare ground for analysis. In this section we discuss transcription and translation of recorded interviews and performances as critical procedural data analysis activities.

We can use many words to explain what it means to have data that is acceptable and whose analysis can provide consistent findings. However, the core issue is integrity that ensures thorough and transparent collection, management and analysis of data. Oral literature fieldwork material is meant to be used both in the original language in which it is performed and the official language of the research. The multiple use of the recorded narratives demands that transcription from the tape remains faithful to the original language. Some of the questions that young researchers grapple with when they come to transcription of the recorded texts are: How much of the text should be transcribed? Who should undertake transcription? What are the major challenges to transcription and how can they be addressed? Answers to these questions lie in introducing transcription protocol to oral literature research. Although there is no universal transcription format that would be adequate for all types of qualitative data collection approaches, settings, or theoretical frameworks, some practical considerations can help researchers prepare transcripts (Drisko 1998:7). Awareness and use of transcription guidelines should help researchers systematically organize and then analyze textual data, regardless of the analytical techniques and tools used. Further, transcription guidelines assist in achieving a high level of certainty that transcripts were generated systematically and consistently.

Transcription can be considered within two categories: full or partial transcription. Full transcription refers to word for word transcription, including an attempt to capture the non-verbal elements related to the performed text. Partial transcription, entails either providing a summary of the performance or interview or transcribing segments of performances or interviews identified for analysis. Strauss and Corbin (1990), in justifying selective transcription, contend that texts selected for transcription should take into account the analytical contribution they will provide to the overall study because, "the level of transcription is supposed to complement the level of the analysis" (31). The main weakness of partial transcription in a performance-related research project is that the text may not be acceptable as it will lose its colour, individuality and oral character. Partial transcription is also limited and has the tendency to transcribe the voice of the artist or interviewee only, leaving out the interviewer. Oral literature scholars at times employ this approach. This selective approach, can be misleading because it tells us nothing about the questions that elicited the response. In the absence of a researcher's contribution to the conversation, we end up judging the respondent out of context. It is therefore advisable to include the questions as well as the answers during transcription. Admittedly, this is a daunting assignment but which is necessary to maintain the research hygiene we mentioned earlier on.

Before the commencement of the data collection process, it is necessary to discuss transcription guidelines with the fieldwork team and make necessary adjustments as the study may demand. It is also important to know who will transcribe, qualifications, when they will do it and how. If it is decided that the local research assistants will handle both interviewing and transcription matters, then they need to be informed of this additional assignment prior to interviewing. Studies have proved that it is easier for researchers to transcribe the data they recorded in the field "because they are most able to remember the context and resolve any bits of the tape which may seem unclear" (*Giving Voice* 16). A number of my research assistants have always wondered why I insist on a tedious full transcription process instead of partial transcription employed in other disciplines and why I remain adamant on word for word transcription instead of free transcription straight from the tapes. At times they think my intention is to punish them. Some students have often approached me to allow them to hire local people to assist them with transcription, a request I have always discouraged, especially when students are fluent in the language of the performance. Determined to have it their way, such researchers do make a second proposal, to be allowed to by-pass transcription by translating straight from the sound files to

English, which is the research language. They peg their requests on the logic that even if they transcribe in the local language, it is them to translate the same texts again into English. So, why not save time and energy? It sounds economical and persuasive.

Although it is possible and economical to translate directly from the tape into the official or national language, I have never allowed my students/research assistants to experiment with this method because it raises several methodological questions that can easily compromise the integrity of the texts translated. Further researchers need to experience transcription and translation separately. The experiences from the two research activities are not the same. In oral literature research, the standard procedure is to subject an entire recording to full transcription. The researcher ensures that an audio-tape is transcribed in its entirety in order to provide a verbatim account of the performance context and interviewing process that follows. The transcripts should include elisions, mispronunciations, slang, grammatical errors, nonverbal sounds and background noises. Assisting transcribers to know what you want included ensures that all transcripts are prepared in a standardized manner and can better provide us with a consistently prepared and comparable textual record. As l encourage full transcription of data collected, I am not blind to the fact that my proposal may only apply to performance based studies and not data in other disciplines especially in social and natural sciences where partial transcription is the norm.

I stress the importance of full transcription as the foundation for meaningful data analysis in oral literature research. I insist that transcription is not limited to meaningful sounds from the tapes, it also includes laughs, sighs, silences and gestures. My insistence on full transcription should not mislead a fieldworker to assume that transcription can recreate an original performance in totality. However meticulous we are in following the procedures, transcription can never be perfect because, as Finnegan observes, there are aspects of performances that may never conform to transcription protocol. What may never be translated include "the poetics; humour; a play between different linguistic registers or vocabulary; stylistic qualities; multi-levels of meaning, perhaps directed to different audiences; connotation; imagery and culturally specific allusion" (Finnegan 190).

Steinar Kvale, echoing Finnegan, also points out that, transcripts 'are not the rock-bottom data of interview research but artificial constructions from an oral to written mode of communication' (163). For example, a researcher must make choices regarding whether a textual document should include non-linguistic observations such as facial expressions and body language; be transcribed verbatim; and identify specific speech patterns, vernacular expressions, intonations, or emotions. Emerson, Fretz, and Shaw (1995) also concede that a transcript can never produce a verbatim record of discourse, given the ongoing interpretive and analytical decisions that are made (9). Full transcription may also not reflect the authentic text because the recording of data is highly perspectival.

Transcriptions often erase the context along with some crucial nonverbal data. What you "see" in a transcription is inescapably selective. A critical theorist sees different things than a deconstructivist or a symbolic interactionist does (Miles and Huberman, 56). The realization that a fieldworker may never achieve the ultimate quest in transcription has made Poland and Pederson to advice fieldworkers "to settle on what is transcribed because despite all best intentions, the textual data will never fully encompass all that takes place during an interview" (294). The argument advanced against essentialization of transcription does not in any way invalidate the need to maintain fidelity to the original performance to narrow the gap between the actual performance and the performance as frozen on paper. Though difficult, it is possible to exploit the full resources of language to make words alive with feelings close to an actual performance.

Transcripts facilitate analysis by including appropriate labelling and content-related information. Regardless of the analytical approach or tools used, we find it useful to include a transcription header with basic information about interview participants. The number and categories of participants may vary from one interview to another, but the key players will unavoidably be present. The transcription header should include an interviewee profile and other essential information as indicated below:

Header details:

- Interviewee
- Age
- Ethnic/racial/faith background
- Educational background
- Gender
- Site/Location

- Date of Interview
- Interviewer
- Transcribers and Translator
- Audience

The above list includes some of the information a researcher may be interested in to aid analysis after the interview. This is an area where a researcher may not avoid basic statistics in terms of the number of respondents within a certain category from age-group to livelihoods.

Once practiced almost exclusively by anthropologists, collecting data in one language and presenting the findings in another is now increasingly common among researchers in the humanities, especially in cultural studies. As scholarship in African oral literature continues to generate interest, a considerable number of theses, dissertations and funded-research projects concern studies which involve moving between languages, sometimes even from the very first steps of the research endeavour like rapport creation. Moving between languages can take different forms. For example, taking English as the language in which the research is to be reported, an English-speaking researcher might conduct an interview in a language other than English like *Dholuo* (a Nilotic language); the researcher interviews in her primary language which is not English; in this case, the researcher and participants are 'fully and fluently bilingual - they slip between the two languages during the interview' (Rossman and Rallis, 161).

Another scenario is where the researcher is only good in English and completely ignorant about *Dholuo*, the language of the performance. The researcher in this case relies totally on the *Dholuo* speaking local assistant to communicate with the artists, facilitate performances, give perspectives to the performances, transcribe and translate the texts. The question that should bother a researcher in this scenario is 'whose text is it? and whose analysis is it?' When collecting data in one language and presenting the findings in another, researchers have to make a number of transcription and translation-related decisions. He or she has to decide on what to do with words which exist in one language but not in another, concepts which are not equivalent in different cultures and idiomatic expressions. Differences among languages in grammatical and syntactical structures are also issues which call for very specific decisions. These decisions along with factors such as, who the researcher or her translators are and what they 'know' have a direct impact on the quality of the findings of the research and the ensuing analysis of the data. These observations justify having a translation protocol in which translation issues, together with emergent issues are anticipated and handled carefully. Factors which affect the quality of translation in oral literature research include:

- Quality of sound data
- Richness of field notes
- Quality of transcription
- Availability of time
- Linguistic competence of the translator in both languages
- Translator's knowledge of the culture of the people under study
- Experience of those involved in the translation, and

• Level of compensation

There is a need for oral literature fieldworkers, who have to translate data from one language to another, to be explicit in describing their choices and decisions, translation procedures and the resources used. One of the early decisions that researchers are asked to make when translating participants' words is whether to go for a 'literal' or 'free' translation of their texts.

In literature, literal translation, or direct translation, is the representation of a text from one language to another "word-for-word" instead of conveying the sense of the original discourse. It is guided by the strict faithfulness to the form of the source language. In many cases, we realize that a translation is factual when a translation does not precisely convey the sense, as it appeared in the original text. This kind of translation can perhaps be seen as doing more justice to what participants have said and 'make one's readers understand the foreign mentality better' (Honig, 17). This approach, though scientific and most preferred by linguists has the potential to reduce the readability of the text, which in turn tests readers' patience and even ability to understand the flow of information. It also has the tendency to distort meanings, especially idioms and the general cultural heritage of a people. This emanates from the fact that language is highly cultural and what a vocabulary means in one language does not have to be close to what a similar vocabulary means in another language. Further, in other languages there is tendency to use many words to express an idea which has only one word in the partner language and *vice versa*. To an extent, this form of translation renders communication syntactically and semantically unintelligible.

Researchers who decide to go for the free translation, on the other hand, need to think of the risk they expose themselves to. There is high likelihood that this kind of translation imposes meanings favoured by the translator that may not have actually been communicated in the text. Rubin and Rubin emphasize the need to create quotations that 'read well,' since even in one's own language, editing quotations always involves the risk of misrepresenting the meaning of the conversational partner (273).

On a number of occasions, I have had to rely on interpreters during oral literature fieldwork. This has meant that I communicate to the target audience through a linguistic intermediary. I have always known that this method has its limitations so I have always tried to make myself clearer to limit the communication gap that is obviously threatening. Honestly speaking, I have not always been successful. Even with the best of efforts, the use of interpreters in research cannot be free of challenges. The situation gets even more complicated when one is conducting research in a community where communicating with intermediaries in the language of research is, in itself, a problem. H. P Phillips identifies 'three basic problems which arise from the use of interpreters as: the interpreter's effect on the informant; the interpreter's effect on the communicative process; the interpreter's effect on the translation' (297). Focusing on the interpreter's effect on translation, Temple argues that researchers who use translators need to acknowledge their dependence on them 'not just for words but to a certain extent for perspective'

(608). In doing so, researchers need to constantly discuss and 'debate' conceptual issues with their translators in order to ensure that conceptual equivalence has been achieved (616). These discussions should be captured in the notes as part of the research data.

Researchers need to be aware that the translation process usually requires skills, time and effort on their part and can present various types of problems, some of which may not be completely overcome. More importantly, however, researchers need to keep in mind that translation-related decisions have a direct impact on the validity of the research and its report. In those cases where the researcher and the translator are the same person the quality of translation is influenced by factors such as: the autobiography of the researcher-translator; the researcher's knowledge of the language, the culture of the people researched and the researcher's fluency in the language of the write-up (Vulliamy, 166).

When the researcher and the translator are not the same person, the quality of translation is influenced mainly by the competence, the autobiography and what Temple calls 'the material circumstances' of the translator that is the position the translator holds in relation to the researcher (610). How then does a researcher who is locked off from the source language ensure that transcription has been faithfully done and that translation retains the spirit and letter of the transcription? Transcription protocol referred to earlier creates a system that regulates transcription and ensures that correct procedures are followed. Having interviewers do the translation, as mentioned before, is another safeguard.

In cases where a researcher has reason to doubt the competence of a translator, it is advisable that some of the texts are sampled and given to an independent expert to conduct back translation. This is a process through which a text originally translated from the source language to the language of research is returned back to its source. By discussing the two versions of the same interview, a researcher is able to assess how close the first translation was to the performance. If the gap is wide, a new translation is done.

Conducting fieldwork on the changing nature of moranism among the Samburu of the Northern Kenya between 2004 and 2007, I learnt that in as much as functional translation meets the practical needs of a researcher, it limits usage of the collected texts. The texts were transcribed word-for-word by local assistants competent in the Samburu language. The translation from Samburu/Kiswahili to English was also done by the transcribers in consultation with research assistants. As opposed to the transcription that was literal, translation of the texts was purely functional with the primary focus on content and style. The translated versions were used strictly to convey meaning rather than structure (Wasamba 2009, 148).

The texts, in their transcription, left out important aspects of the performances that the audience may never know. The various body movements, facial expressions and dances which energised the performances as well as the interjections by inspired members of the audience can only be viewed in VCDs. However, due to financial constraints and technical lapses, not all performances were captured on VCDs or DVDs. The few performances recorded using the audio visual cameras were, unfortunately, not of the best quality. This experience reveals that, even with the best of intentions and skills, capturing the authentic oral performance using audio visual equipment is quite challenging unless the researcher has a back-up professional film crew. Poor recording automatically compromises transcription, translation and ultimately data analysis.

Our discussion of the centrality of transcription and translation indicates that fieldworkers must disclose all translation-related decisions to put readers/peers in the picture. Good practice in ethnographic research insists that reports of fieldwork include a detailed explanation of the translation-related issues, problems and decisions involved at the different stages of the research continuum. In addition, researchers need to describe the circumstances within which translation took place and the techniques they used during the translation process. Similarly, if the research involved the use of translators, readers need to be informed about who those people were, their expertise in translation and the specific role they played in each stage of the research enterprise. I am giving much attention to transcription and translation processes because they not only facilitate data analysis but are part and parcel of the data analysis. If handled professionally, they make it possible for the data to be analyzed, interpreted, packaged and disseminated in good time.

Data Analysis

One need not belabour the point that research data does not stand alone. Data neighbour analysis which pervades all phases of the research activity. Data analysis, as we have explained, is never a one-off activity. It runs throughout the research circle from the time a researcher makes observations, records them in field notes, selects and groups the notes into analytic categories, and finally develops explicit theoretical propositions. Viewed in this way, analysis is at once inductive and deductive, like someone who is simultaneously creating and solving a puzzle (Emerson, M. Robert et. al. 144). Alicia J Rouveral advocates involving one's interviewees in the subsequent analysis of the interviews, arguing that authority should be shared beyond the interview itself (Pollock 25). Rouveral's participatory analysis is in synch with Okoth Okombo, who argues that human communities "are not just communities of naïve actors; they are also communities of analysts, who reflect and pass judgment on their own actions" (22).

The foregoing argument strongly indicates that fieldwork in oral literature should capture indigenous theory of criticism to facilitate community responsive evaluation of the performances. Grounded theory and ethno-methodology respond to this need. The constant comparative method integral to grounded theory is presented as a manual step-by-step analysis that entails inductive category coding based on "units of meaning" of textual data, refinement of categories, exploration of relationships and patterns across categories leading to data integration or sense-making (Maykut and Morehouse, 126). Grounded theory is distinguished in terms of reporting approaches, philosophical assumptions, data collection activities including the logic of sampling, data analysis strategies and representation, rhetorical structures and terms about verification (Bong Sharon, 6). Applying grounded theory to data analysis, therefore means allowing the data to "speak for itself rather than subjecting it to the existing theoretical frameworks (Welsh, 5). Reviewing a set of field notes, interviews, journals and photographs, and to open them up meaningfully, while keeping the relations between the parts intact, is what data analysis is all about. It involves how one differentiates and combines the data retrieved and the reflections one makes about this information.

People make and use stories to interpret the world. They perform life. Performance comprises the rhythms and cadences, repetitions and intonations, the use of particular speech forms such as anecdote or reported speech, the use of the dialect, as well as volume, tone and speed. Without attention to these features in research we risk flattening 'the emotional content of the speech down to the supposed equanimity and objectivity of the written document (Abrams, 19). Narrative is used to 'translate knowing into telling' (White, 5). Analysis common to verbal arts, therefore, entails the identification and interpretation of the ways in which people use stories to interpret the world. It involves the identification of verbal or written structures within texts by means of linguistic or literary analysis.

Ethnographic research methods employed in oral literature field work are descriptive in nature. In conducting data analysis, we assume that the field researcher has collected primary data in the form of field notes, research journal, voice or video recordings of interviews and other materials in the field that can aid interpretation like photographs of significant landscapes, cultural objects or personalities. All this information is reduced to words at the data processing level. The unit of analysis is therefore word or groups of words. Due to the massive data that qualitative research generates, analysis, as elaborated by Tufte, unavoidably involves synthesis, filtration, selection, discrimination and integration, which calls for a set of analytic categories.

Data analysis involves walking through multiple data sources such as photographs, recordings, artefacts and diaries to sieve meaning from them, condense them, order them and categorize them. In the process of sieving, sifting, shifting and condensing, we assign codes to the data; identify similarities and differences in the clusters of information before us, isolate patterns that stand out and come up with generalizations that respond to our research question. Coding refers to the process through which raw data is retrieved, sorted and organized into either preconceived or emergent communicative categories. It entails data reduction which involves focusing, simplifying, abstracting and transforming the processed data. In deciding what to leave in, what to highlight, what to report first and last, what to interconnect, and what main ideas are important, analytic choices are being made continuously (Miles and Huberman, 8).

Coding in Oral Literature

In conducting data analysis in oral literature, coding is hardly applied with the mathematical rigor of social science. This is because majority of oral literature researchers are not exposed to social science research methods where training in coding is conducted. It is also argued that fieldworkers have always interpreted textual data in oral literature without bending to the dictates of social scientists. Consequently, a number of researchers with literary background aver that through continued readings of the source material and vigilance over one's presuppositions, one can reach the "essence" of an account (Miles, and Huberman, 8).

I encourage a paradigm that stays focused on analytical processes and products without valorizing particular approaches to coding as *sine qua non*. What should concern fieldworkers is: What they are looking for in data, and how they can get it in such a way that it meets their expectations and the threshold of a respectable research undertaking. Regardless of whether one uses coding, narrative analysis or discourse analysis, researchers should prove the claims they make. In humanities, this has been achieved through content analysis which is a methodical technique for condensing many words of text into fewer content categories based on explicit rules of data organization. Content analysis systematically identifies "specified characteristics of messages" (Holsti, 1969, 14) and enables researchers to sift through large volumes of data with relative ease (Gao, 1996). Coding, as applied in social sciences, should not be dangled as the mantra of qualitative data analysis. Literary critics have analyzed volumes of data for centuries without schemata of codes. The debate should not be reduced to whether categorization is important or not in analysis. There is no doubt about that. The question is what is meant by coding and how to go about it. This is where researchers in humanities part with their counterparts in social sciences. The latter believe that coding must be mathematical while the former thinks that coding does not have to be mechanical, it can be achieved by grasping the 'essence' of the information.

Some of the challenges faced by qualitative researchers include the labour-intensiveness of data collection that extends to months and even years, frequent data overload, the distinct possibility of researcher bias, the time demands of processing and coding data, the adequacy of sampling when only a few cases can be managed, the generality of findings, the credibility and quality of conclusions, and their utility in the world of policy and action (Miles and Huberman, 2).

Textualization in Verbal Art

The process of data collection and data analysis in oral literature field research settings is characterized by 'push and pull' tension between 'traditionists' out to protect oral literature from imagined encroachment by 'outsiders' and expansionist ethnographers passionate to 'colonize' the neighbouring disciplines, oral literature included. When Wole Soyinka and Jan Janheinz lament lack of theoretical audacity in oral literature scholarship in Africa, they are not only raising questions on how we engage with the recorded texts, but also the process that delivers texts for analysis. Muana is then correct to ask:

> So what should provide the basis of analyses in the study of verbal art? Is it text or context? What is the text? Is it the sanitized, disembodied transcript of the spoken or sung word that is produced from the publishing house to readers? If this is not the whole text, then where does text end and where does context begin? Who determines context? How is context related to text? Can the interface between text and context be described? (40)

Tension between literary critics and ethnographers is symptomatic of the cold war between textualists and contextualists, decontextualists and recontextualists, and the objectivists and subjectivists in oral literature research. While reasons advanced sound plausible by the opposing camps, the difference seems to be more ideological than literary. Textualization refers to the generic process whereby a researcher translates experience into text (Clifford, 113). The textual school defends the 'age-old' practices of collection and documentation in oral literature field research without using other methodologies from other disciplines. Textualists affirm the centrality of objectivity in research. They argue that researcher's agenda is divorced from the research location and that; the work produced is the product of researcher's own genius.

Lastrucci, C L. in *The Scientific Approach: Basic Principles of the Scientific Method,* supports objectivity in research. He contends that methodology conscious approach to fieldwork demands "a rigorous, impersonal mode of procedure dictated by the demands of logic and objective procedure" (7). Advocates of objectivity further aver that, although fieldwork is crucial, the field remains untouched by the researcher's work. The researcher is only expected to observe the field from a privileged position of "detached impartiality" and that he or she is impervious to influence from those studied in any way. Empiricists, who are devout students of textuality, contend that venturing into contexts, opens floodgates to mediocrity and anarchy in research. Consequently, the integrity of the literary research data and their subsequent analysis cannot be verified because they are merely 'impressionistic' and therefore, 'unscientific'.

Contextualists, on the other hand, argue that text-centred analyses of fieldwork data are problematic. Informed by the works of Bronislaw Malinowski, and later Milman Parry and Albert Lord, 'contextualists' argue that what text-centred studies have referred to as 'the text' is communicative action which signals aspects of cultural and social order from which discourse emerges (Muana 41). Far from being explanatory, context is in itself seen as a system of interpretation because, it is argued, text cannot be analyzed *in vacuo* (Georges, 37).

Re-contextualization, a paramount concern for oral literature fieldworkers, involves grounding representations to new audiences in the modes of presentation occurring in a "natural" context. This ensures that field research and scholarship in oral literature reaches a wider audience. Fieldwork, by employing re-contextualization, succeeds in making tradition to be understood as "part of modernity rather than a part of it" (Baron and Spitzer ix). The need to use text as core substance of research cannot be downplayed. Nevertheless, the fact that the study is conducted by a human being, among other human beings within a cultural setting, implies that mediation between the text and context is not only unavoidable, but necessary and desirable. The following questions can help steer the debate between textualists and contextualists to rapprochement: Is it realistic to divorce ourselves from our research? Is it intellectually honest to separate ourselves, to silence our voices as researchers within our research processes and reports? And, if we choose to include our own voices in our research report, how are we to do so without the risk of introspection or self-indulgence?

Fieldwork in oral literature is persuasive, purposive, positional and political which makes absolute objectivity a pipe-dream. Distanced and objective stance in fieldwork is dishonest. To ignore yourself as part of data distorts your findings – you are the researcher who selects particular details, records informant's voices, chooses what to leave in and what to take out, and decides how to write about the "particular" as it "illuminates" the human condition you studied (Chiseri-Strater Elizabeth & Bonnie Stone Sunstein, 39). Goffman Erving (1989), in particular, insists that field research involves "subjecting yourself, your own body and your own personality, and your own social situation to the set of contingencies that play upon a set of individuals, so that you can physically and ecologically penetrate their circle of response to their social situation, or their work situation, or their ethnic situation (125). Clearly, ethnographic immersion precludes conducting field research as a detached, passive observer; the field researcher can only get close to the lives of those studied by actively participating in their day-to-day affairs (Emerson, M. Robert et. al. 2).

No field researcher can be completely neutral, detached observer, outside and independent of the observed phenomena. Rather, as the ethnographer engages in the lives and concerns of those studied his perspective "is intertwined with phenomenon that does not have objective characteristics independent of the observer's perspective and methods" (Mishler, 10). The field researcher comes to understand others' ways by becoming part of their lives and by learning to interpret and experience events much as they do. The researcher decides where to go, what to look at, what to ask and say, so as to experience fully another way of life and its concerns. Fieldworkers, as Chiseri-Strater Elizabeth & Bonnie Stone Sunstein points out, do not depend on detachment or on the objectivity that comes from stepping out of a culture. They rely on human involvement – their gut reactions or subjective responses to cultural practices (7). Personhood cannot, therefore, be left behind, cannot be left out of the research process (Frankfort-Nachmias, Chava and David Nachmias, 75). Finnegan, in proposing a truce between the warring ideological camps, proposes a cautious but inclusive approach to data collection and analysis in ethnographic research. She observes that fieldworkers should pay attention to the "essential subject matter," which includes; the verbal texts and contexts (Finnegan 26).

Computer-Assisted Qualitative Data Analysis Software

We live in an information rich society. Computers have revolutionized the way we conduct research, analyze data and disseminate ideas. This development promises tangible benefits and palpable dangers that researchers in oral literature must be aware of. Much has been written about the use of computers in qualitative data analysis since the late '80s (Wasamba, 2007a/b). Computer-Assisted Qualitative Data Analysis Software (CAQDAS) has gained popularity in social sciences and humanities. CAQDAS is based on the grounded theory approach to data analysis. This may explain why nearly all software developers for QDA claim to have tools which facilitate theory building from the data. One cannot say with certainty the number of CAQDAS available in the market at any one given time. This is because the number of new software programmes keeps on growing while others are gliding into disuse. Some of the dedicated qualitative data analysis software programmes available in the market are: NVIVO, ATLAS-ti and MAXqda, which are considered as market leaders due to their multiple functions for data analysis. It would be prudent to state this early, that CAQDAS does not promise magic in data analysis. No qualitative data analysis tool eliminates the need for the researcher to think (Jemmont, 2002: 7). The tools of analysis, however technically sound, can only be as effective as one applies them (Wasamba, 19).

CAQDAS, like all new ideas that challenge traditions, have been treated with skepticism and in some cases outright rejection. In literary criticism, many scholars believe that the use of software poses a threat to the craft skills of a long-established research tradition. They wonder how a product of imagination, like good oral poetry performed before a charged audience, can be subjected to the dictates of machines like computers which are incapable of gauging human feelings. They also foresee danger of mediocre analysis produced by doctrinaire allegiance to a mechanical set of procedures in a computer. Protectionists of "pure literature" also advance a conspiracy theory that CAQDAS has an implicit theory which favours social scientists and gives a raw deal to humanities, especially literature. Literary critics are not alone in suspecting mischief in QDA tools. Other social scientists also express concern that the software may "guide" researchers in a particular direction (Seidel, 1991). Besides, it distances the researcher from the data and forces qualitative data into quantitative analysis thereby creating homogeneity in methods (Barry 1998).

It cannot be denied that compared to the manual methods, computer aided analysis facilitates faster, near-accurate and transparent data analysis process, and in so doing, succeeds in painting a reliable, comprehensive kaleidoscope of the data field (Morison and Moir 1998). The most unique feature of CAQDAS, however, is their ability to effectively categorize and annotate a wide variety of data, in particular, textual data thereby enabling researchers to adduce evidence to back up their claims. If, for example, a researcher has a number of interview transcripts, field notes, case notes, newspaper articles, focus group discussion (FGD) transcripts or even pictures, audio and audio-visual files, a good computer software programme assists with managing, shaping and analyzing this type of data within a short time and with minimum labour.

It is important to look at the advantages that the computer assisted software programmes avail to researchers. Thereafter, we can also evaluate the challenges that the new technology introduces. The programmes are good at organising research data; lends credibility to research methodology; facilitates documentation and integration of analyst's observations; offers analysts flexibility in managing data and encourages use of manual analysis to address gaps the software cannot deal with. The software programmes do not make the use of manual data analysis obsolete. Indeed, they encourage it to fill the gaps that computers cannot capture. I reiterate Hamilton Jemmott's observation that computer based data analysis, for example, does not eliminate the need for the researcher to think and manually engage with the data. The analyst has to construct and account for the data and the methods and processes of analysis. The search engines of these programmes cannot capture the contexts in which certain words are used, especially in performances which are fertile grounds for paralinguistic features, idioms, humour, imagery and figurative language. A researcher should counter-check the searches manually to capture other words or experiences that could have been left out by the machine.

The challenges posed by over-relying on computer guided analysis of qualitative data include the gap between expectation and reality – analysts new to CAQDAS expect miracles with data and get disappointed when they realize that the software is just a means, not an end in itself. Researchers also discover discrepancy between the marketing of the software and performance. Analysts get disappointed when they realize that the lofty words used to market the versatility of the software conceal the bitter reality that the efficacy of the tool is exaggerated and that the software can only deliver to one who matches its level of sophistication. There is also a gap between an analyst's technical capacity and software's technical requirements. There is also lack of expertise in the selection of an appropriate CAQDAS.

Many researchers selecting software do not have the expertise to make informed assessments of the different tools thus; decisions are based on colleagues' recommendations or trial and error. Oral literature scholars in addition encounter challenges when it comes to the analysis of style in recorded narratives. CAQDAS programmes are more content based and do not provide tools for analyzing the aesthetic components of a performance. Analysis of rhythm, dramatic bodily movements, tonal variations, metaphor, symbolism, humour, and other techniques is not directly catered for. The software developers leave the burden of capturing these insights to the analysts. Furthermore, the cost of good software is too expensive for many researchers and institutions. Nevertheless, compared to the benefits mentioned earlier on, these challenges are surmountable.

Once data analysis is conducted, information should be packaged in a research reports that reveals the entire journey of the quest. Below is a model of how a research report looks like.

Report Outline

- Preliminaries
- Title page
- Contents
- Acknowledgements
- Background to the community studied
- Introduction to the project
- Preparation

- Fieldwork methodology
- Oral artists and their backgrounds
- The texts recorded
- The artist
- The text in the local language
- The translation in English/Kiswahili
- Analysis and interpretation
- Conclusion
- The major findings
- Opportunities for future research in the area
- The challenges faced in the field
- Strategies used to address the challenges
- Recommendations on how to make the future research more productive
- The End Matter
- Appendices
- Photos
- Interview schedule
- Interview transcripts
- Release forms
- Letter of authorization
- Works Cited List

This outline is just a guide. In many cases, a researcher will come up with a new format for presenting the research report. What is important is that the report should capture the entire journey of the research from inception to analysis, interpretation, findings and dissemination.

Fieldwork Ethics, Challenges and Strategies

Oral Literature fieldworkers, like other folklorists, work closely with people who, in most cases, do not come from the same cultural, social and economic backgrounds as the researcher. And even if by chance a fieldworker finds himself/herself in a familiar environment, the requirements of research redefine the relationship between a researcher and his/her community, kith and kin. The main challenge a researcher faces is how to accommodate the delicate interests of various stakeholders in a fieldwork project so that their diverse energies can be harnessed for the good of the discipline. A fieldworker interacts with colleagues, students, sponsors, local administration, informants and local assistants in the host communities. Depending on the issues at hand, dealing with each of these groups exposes a fieldworker to various ethical dilemmas and other related fieldwork challenges.

It is important that a fieldworker anticipates some of these issues so that remedial measures are contemplated before they occur. It is pragmatic to state this early that ethical issues in research cannot be theorised. They emerge in particular circumstances to particular individuals and may never be replicated in other studies. It is incumbent upon the fieldworker to build on the experiences of others but remain keen to identify ethical issues generated through personal experiences in the field. Unlike in the medical field and biological research, ethical considerations have not been taken seriously in oral literature research. This is based on the assumption that the informants are not exposed to any harm. Whereas oral literature research informants are not likely to suffer harm like guinea-pigs in a medical research, they are still exposed to different kinds of harm and must be protected. This chapter demonstrates the centrality of ethical considerations in oral literature fieldwork. It also addresses some common challenges in a fieldwork situation and proposes strategies for dealing with them.

Ethics and Oral Literature

In September 2008, I presented a paper entitled "Ethnic Identities and Ethical Dilemmas in Fieldwork," at the national symposium on the role of oral literature in promoting peace and national cohesion. The symposium was organised by the Kenya Oral Literature Association (KOLA) to facilitate the healing process in Kenya after the civil strife that engulfed the country following the disputed presidential elections in December 2007. The paper was inspired by the disturbing allegation that some cultural scholars might have participated directly or indirectly in fanning ethnic hatred and near-genocide at the behest of politicians or ethnic communities. I challenged fellow fieldworkers to conduct self reflection to save fieldwork in the post-conflict confusion and suspicion. I asked:

To what extent does ethnic conflict affect the design of oral literature fieldwork? What is required of a fieldworker in a civil conflict situation? How can fieldworkers resist the magnetic pull of negative ethnicity? Are fieldworkers allowed to link research to advocacy for peaceful co-existence in a conflicted society? What kind of truth is truthful in a conflict-ridden fieldwork locale? Considering that civil strife imposes severe constraints in data collection, is deception of research participants acceptable? Can a fieldworker spy for the government to provide useful information that can stop violence and save lives? And, what should oral literature fieldworkers do to come up with some benchmarks to guide professional conduct of researchers in ethnically divided society? (Wasamba 2009, 195-6)

A number of participants responded to my paper positively arguing that it exposed the predicament of fieldworkers in an ethnically divided society. Some participants were, however, of the view that ethical issues are not a priority in oral literature research because they are not clear and may end up limiting researchers by creating unnecessary fear of breaking the rules. They were also apprehensive that once ethical standards are introduced to fieldwork practice, a few individuals may abuse the code to limit other researchers' freedom by elevating themselves to 'high priests' of regulations. They are not alone. Traditionally it has been assumed that ethics are matters of biomedical research where one deals with human subjects exposed to greater health risks through experimentation. Such scholars perceive ethics in research as abstract and intimidating set of 'don't dos'. They dread codes of ethics as a set of rigid injunctions to be ruthlessly enforced. They hardly consider codes of ethics as a reflection of desire born out of professional commitment by fieldworkers to respect the rights of others, fulfil research obligations, avoid harm and enhance benefits to those they interact with in their calling as researchers. Participants opposed to strengthening ethical practice in fieldwork were advancing the argument that ethical matters have no place in oral literature research and should be left to medical scientists.

I was surprised by the spirited attempt to avoid addressing ethical concerns. I wondered whether a fieldworker has any choice when it comes to ethical considerations in the field. James N. Hill in his article "The Committee on Ethics: Past, Present, and Future", indicates that a fieldworker cannot avoid dealing with ethical issues. The field is like a mine field. It is full of challenges that demand that a fieldworker makes difficult decisions in terms of resolving disputes, handling relationship matters, authorization and corruption. The argument that ethics has no place in oral literature scholarship suggests that fieldwork has no risks or deputes that require avoidance or amicable resolution. There are always disputes over ownership of recorded texts, confidentiality, corruption, informed consent, anonymity of informants, payment of informants, research permit and relationships between researchers and their informants. These cases often introduce ethical concerns that a researcher cannot ignore.

There is an emerging realization within the oral literature fraternity that regardless of the topic of research, ideological leaning or theoretical orientation, no fieldworker can ignore ethical considerations in their work. This is because "moral and ethical decisions occur at all stages of the research, from the selection of the topic, area or population, sponsor and source of funding, to publication of findings and disposal of data" (Akeroyd, 134). Miles, & Huberman, concur with Akeroyd that ethical concerns are unavoidable to a researcher who is not asleep. Any fieldworker who is not asleep weighs moral and ethical choices constantly. A fieldworker keeps on asking:

> Is my project really worth doing? Do people really understand what they are getting into? Am I exploiting people with my "innocent" questions? What about their privacy? Do respondents have a right to see my report? What good is anonymity if people and their colleagues can easily recognize themselves in a case study? When they do, might it hurt or damage them in some way? What do I do if I observe a harmful behaviour in my cases? Who will benefit and who will lose as a result of my study? Who owns the data, and who owns the report? (288).

Ethical questions precede the research, become intense during the study and remain active long after the study is done. It is based on the question "What if?" A keen fieldworker will ponder over issues specific to her or his study. One may be keen on intrusion: In what ways will the study intrude, come closer to people than they want? How is it possible to demarcate the line separating an honest interview with intrusion? How will information received be protected from access to unauthorized persons? How identifiable are the individuals and organizations studied? Who owns my field notes, photographs and analyses? Is it myself, my research organization or the clients who funded the research I did? This may sound a simple matter until a dispute arises at the end of the study. How do researchers ensure that the 'well-motivated, honest, humane, and compassionate involvement of fieldworkers with informants is not condemned by later generations of researchers as patronizing, exploitative, and corrupt'? (Proschan F., 149).

Ethics and Reciprocity

In my research experience, 1 have gathered that communities hold researchers in high esteem. Fieldworkers attract respect due to their interest in detail, patience and empathy. Respect accorded researchers working with communities come at a price – expectation of an honest, respectful and beneficial treatment. Researchers, at times, violate this trust by ignoring the host communities in what they do: They do not explain what they do, how they do it and how the work benefits them as researchers. Oral literature fieldworkers are not innocent in their research activities as they would want peers and other research participants to believe. In a bold discussion of the relationship between a fieldworker and those studied, Hawes observes that there is need to acknowledge the debt owed to those studied:

> As much as we try to get away from the uncomfortableness of it, the fundamental fact of being a folklorist is that we earn our living by various manipulations of other people's creative products or information. It just comes with the territory. We are not alone in this, of course. Literary scholars, music critics, and art historians as

well depend for their very existence upon the creative productivity
of other people." (Hawes 68)

Hawes adds that the relationship between the researcher and the
researched provides a titled landscape in which the researched
are disadvantaged. This calls for a guarantee that the advantage
enjoyed by researchers is not to be misused. It is research ethics
that secures such a promise of fair treatment. Hawes' honest
acknowledgement of the debt owed to informants is corroborated
by Miles & Huberman, who contend that, compared to
informants who hardly get tangible benefits, researchers are
often paid; they usually enjoy their work and learn from it; they
may get a dissertation out of it; their papers, articles, and books
not only contribute to "science" but can also bring them
recognition, royalties, new funding, and career advancement
(291).

Omondi Tawo the Bard

Reflecting on my research experience in 1996 with an oral praise
poet called Omondi Tawo, living in one of the slums of Nairobi
city, I concur with Hawe that fieldworkers enjoy advantages
that can easily be abused if ethical concerns are not respected.
The situation of my respondent at the time of the interview
cannot picture the disadvantage any better. Charles Omondi
Tawo (1943 - 2000) was born in Alego, Siaya District of Nyanza
Province in Kenya. His father was a bard. He therefore had the
privilege of being apprenticed by his father soon after he dropped
out of school. Apart from playing *nyatiti*, Omondi Tawo also
practised as a traditional medicine man. This earned him the

nick-name *nyasaye*, a Luo word for god. He claimed he had powers to heal those who are lovesick, infertile or bewitched. In 1996 when I met him for the first time, it was clear that the legend was fading, and rapidly so. He epitomized an oral artist in grinding poverty. There was obvious difference between his fame and his physical condition. He had two wives and three children, not to mention "countless" mistresses whom he proudly referred to as his female admirers. ...The poet was perpetually drunk and dirty. Food was visibly scarce and privacy a luxury in his house. What struck me most was the fact that the poet was not disturbed by his situation (Wasamba 2004: 3). Informants like Omondi Tawo need assurance that researchers will protect them from abuse and exploitation. Tawo was not in a strong position to bargain. He was ready to perform so long as I assured him that I would give him 'something' at the end for beer. Such experiences dramatize the need to strengthen code of ethics in research to ensure that the deprivation of informants is not used to exploit and intrude into their lives without respectful reciprocal treatment.

Ethics and Accountability

Ethics in fieldwork is addressed by many practitioners such as Denzin and Lincoln (2000), Silverman (1997) and Hammersley and Atkinson (1995). In a detailed discussion of research ethics, Williams and Brydon-Miller, argue that no researcher dealing with human beings can escape accountability and responsibility. Some of the questions they ask include, "What responsibilities do researchers have to help change the material conditions of the participants of their research? What legitimacy do researchers have in representing the experiences of others?" (242). Brown and Sidney are even more explicit in asserting the logic of ethics by asking questions such as: "Who benefits from research? Whose interests are at stake? What are the consequences for participants?" (4). Good Anthony in editor's Forward to Finnegan's *Oral Traditions and the Verbal Arts*, adds his voice to the discourse by expanding debate on ownership of research products: "Who – if anyone- can be said to 'own' the data in question, and what artistic, legal, or financial responsibilities do fieldworkers bear towards those whose verbal performances they 'collect'?" (Finnegan 1992: xi). These questions underscore the primary thesis that research that involves other people can never be a mechanical activity since it is capable of affecting those studied negatively or positively.

Fieldwork territory, according to Hawes, gives researchers undue advantage. Most of the performances and interviews we enjoy, analyze, comment upon, display and organize come from people who are either economically poorer than most academicians or at best less experienced in terms of how to survive using their art in a competitive society like Omondi Tawo. It should make fieldworkers remorseful that while we are too quick to defend what we call "intellectual property rights", we are exploiting good-natured men and women who are too welcoming to safeguard their intangible property.

Akeroyd rightly points out that 'knowledge is not only a source of enlightenment but also of power and property. It entails the power both to harm and to benefit those studied' (134). Social scientists like Hawes insist that all research is exploitative and incurable from ethical transgressions. According to this school, a fieldworker has so much power at his/her disposal that even if we have the most comprehensive codes of ethics that is religiously adhered to, the landscape would remain tilted in favor of the researcher. Given the inevitably asymmetrical relations of power between these parties, and considering the partiality of knowledge and experience, Horner calls on fieldworkers to be empathetic and proactive in addressing ethical issues in field research. Researchers should "ask themselves what would constitute ethically responsible ways of defining, initiating, carrying out, and reporting on their research" (14). Fieldwork ethics challenge researchers to apply affirmative action to restore balance between all research actors. Fieldworkers should be bold to admit that unequal power relations between a fieldworker and informants require that research be used to create awareness that can propel the participants from *gnosis* (awareness) to the level of *praxis* (action). Self-motivated action driven by awareness of one's situation can help those who have been "marginalized to speak for themselves" (Kirsh Gesa and Joy Ritchie 25).

Ethics and Informed Consent

In research ethics, respectful treatment of informants is secured by the principle of informed consent, which is a slippery principle. What is informed consent? What does it imply? What does informed consent, consent to? How does informed consent in anthropology differ from that in other disciplines? (du Toit, B. M., 274). Informed consent in a fieldwork environment means that prospective research informants are fully told about the procedures, benefits and risks involved in the proposed research and are hence adequately enabled to participate based on thorough knowledge. It is a tricky requirement considering that the person who controls the process that leads to an informed consent is an interested party. Depending on the stakes and the willingness of the informant, the researcher can manipulate the situation to get informed consent, anyway. The question is how informed, is an informed consent?

Ethical standards dictate that researchers do not put participants in situations where they may be exposed to risk or harm as a result of their participation. Harm in research can be defined as both physical and psychological. Privacy of informants is paramount and must be protected at all cost. Privacy is insulated by guaranteeing participants confidentiality and anonymity. They are assured that information rendered will not be made available to anyone who is not directly involved in the study. The more demanding standard is the principle of anonymity which in actual fact means that the identities of the informant remain concealed throughout and after the study.

Clearly, the anonymity standard is a stronger guarantee of privacy, which in many cases is difficult to accomplish in a libertarian study. How do you achieve the objective of giving voice to the voiceless by making them anonymous? In an oral literature fieldwork, the intentions of artists and other key informants is always different. They have no problem with being known. Indeed, others seek publicity through research and cannot be stopped by fieldworkers. In an ironic twist some informants end up endangering the researcher by distorting the research purpose to boost their social standing. I had such an experience in 2009. I was conducting research in Teso District, in Western Kenya on ethno-medicine. The area is famous for medicine-men who identify theft suspects by making the culprits eat grass like cows in a public square. These medicine-men are locally called 'grass-eaters,' not because they eat grass, but rather because they make thieves do so.

Once theft is reported, the villagers, especially the suspects are assembled in an open space and served a glass of 'medicine' (herbal cocktail). Immediately a culprit sips that liquid, he or she goes into a delirium and starts eating grass and vegetation around the place aggressively until cured by another concoction from the same medicine-man. I went with my students to study one of the leading grass-eaters in the area. My worry was that he would decline because they are known to be highly secretive. He shocked my colleague and I, when he welcomed the idea and even prepared refreshments for the entire research team. I learnt later that he did it in a bid to gain publicity over local rival medicine-men. Unfortunately, my name was also included in the broadcast. It was announced over the national radio service as a news item that I was working closely with grass-eaters of Teso to stamp out rampant theft. The informant made sure that my name and that of my colleague were mentioned as the researchers working closely with him. I was not impressed. My parents who are staunch Christians and church leaders in our village heard about it from others. They took the message to mean I was being trained to become an expert in that genre. Relatives who know me also started approaching me secretly to show them how to make thieves eat grass. In this particular episode, I remember giving my colleague my camera, since he was standing close to the informant, to take a few shots. When I got my camera back, there was no photo of the event. My colleague apologetically told me that the medicine-man's spell fell over him and immobilized him. He never remembered that he had a camera with him.

Ethical considerations discussed in fieldwork assume that researchers are protected and it is those studied who are at risk. From the Teso episode, it is apparent that, in some cases, a researcher could be more at risk or at a disadvantage in terms of power relations. In an interview event in a witchdoctor's clinic, who is at a disadvantage between a witch dreaded by everybody in the society and a humble scholar? This story brings out the other side of the coin which is never considered when discussing research ethics: Are informants that helpless as suggested? Are fieldworkers that powerful in the community? Who protects fieldworkers after they have protected the informants? Who addresses the trauma and nightmares that fieldworkers go through after interviewing scary informants?

It may surprise many that while conducting fieldwork, investigators have comparatively little power over those who are studied. The environment dictates the balance of power: informants are usually free to leave the situation or to decline to enter interaction. In a point of fact, those who are studied frequently have some power over the investigators, who may depend upon the host community for shelter, food and security. In fieldwork, then, power is shared between investigators and subjects, with subjects having somewhat more power to frustrate research than researchers have to compel them to participate. Subjects control the setting of research and influence the context, with interaction flowing comparatively freely in both directions (Cassell, 31). Frank Proschan concurs with Cassell and asserts that a fieldworker starts his or her fieldwork from a position of disadvantage because no community owes a fieldworker a debt of cooperation, even if he/she happens to come from that particular community. This is simply because the community's priorities will not always coincide with those of the scholar, "whose questions about old songs or the best storyteller does little to ensure there is food on the table or a place to sleep for anyone other than the questioner" (148). Fieldworkers should go to the field aware that they are not the kings of the jungle. They are likely to be minions.

How does a fieldworker deal with an avalanche of goodwill from informants? Fieldworkers are always worried about getting cooperation from informants and community leaders. At times, the opposite happens and fieldworkers are caught flat-footed. What happens when you get an over-enthusiastic artist who will never let you go, even after pleading your case that the research is over? Over-zealous respondents should be managed well to keep the study on course, or else, a fieldworker may suffer the predicament of Mrs. Hawes student who resorted to literally running away from his former respondent who would simply not let him have peace long after the interview:

> When I was teaching years ago, I had a student who did an excellent term paper based upon some folk curing beliefs he had collected from an old lady in the neighbourhood. At the end of the semester, he voiced a complaint, "You taught me all about how to collect, Mrs. Hawes. What you didn't teach me was how to stop collecting. That old lady lives on my block, and every night when I come home,

she runs out on the porch and says, 'Hey, boy, I just remembered another one! I keep explaining to her that my project is all finished, but she just won't stop, and I'm starting to go up the alley when I go home just so I won't run into her." (Hawes 68)

In 2001, I coordinated a needs assessment survey in a number of districts in Kenya. I formed five teams of graduate students from local universities. Majority of the research assistants were conducting systematic fieldwork for the first time. The teams went to the remote parts of the country where they stayed with the communities collecting qualitative data for three weeks. In their reports, nearly all teams observed that even though the study was quite demanding, the respect community members accorded them as researchers motivated them to carry on. For instance, they reported that they got the titles of 'officers', a prestigious designation normally reserved for senior civil servants in Kenya. In addition, community members were generous to researchers. They not only volunteered information sought for but also gifts and food, even when their situations did not warrant such generosity.

One day, a researcher visited a village to conduct a focus group discussion (FGD) with members of a women's group in Kisumu West District, and was shocked to find an elaborate ceremony organised for the 'officer from Nairobi' (the fieldworker). Although the interview was to take half an hour, the women group had prepared a handwritten programme for a whole day with two tea breaks, a lunch break and a repertoire of songs, all at their own expense. The young researcher did not know what to do. He had been trained on rapport creation to overcome resistance by host communities. He had not imagined meeting a community that is too willing to participate in research. Floods of goodwill from the hosts sent him into a state of confusion. Suddenly, the young researcher started debating on what to do: was it right to snub the villagers after spending their time and meagre resources preparing a party for him? Was it professional to spend a whole day with one group merry-making whereas other appointments were waiting? Could the provision of food and other gifts compromise his observations in any way? How was he to reciprocate this kind gesture with his meagre allowance?

Managing Expectations

Balanced with inexplicable generosity are cases of high expectations on the fieldworker. Community members oftentimes mistake researchers for government policy makers or donors' representatives. When they host a researcher, they are excited because the government's agent has finally come down to them and will address their immediate, and if possible, long term needs. This partly explains why the villagers' expectations on the fieldworker are always quite high. Before long, a fieldworker starts receiving delegations from the community in the evening seeking information or favours on various issues ranging from the state of politics in the city to education and relationship matters. Majority are keen on education and the future of their children. They want their children to be employed in the capital city, bursary for their children in high schools, admission to national universities and assistance with selection into prestigious disciplines like Medicine, Law and Engineering even if they have lower grades. Some cases are so genuine and indeed so touching like single parents struggling with failing health requesting for assistance to either buy painkillers or food for sick orphans.

In other cases, depending on the age, gender and status of the researcher, there are also marriage proposals. A researcher, therefore, needs to be extra cautious to avoid giving the false impression that he or she can ameliorate the challenges faced by the community. Nevertheless, fieldworkers have to contend with the old adage that 'nothing comes out of nothing'. The law of reciprocity applies to all human interactions and researchers are not exempted. Fieldworkers are human beings empathetic to the situations of their hosts. This affords them latitude to respond to the needs of the host communities within the reasonable limits of research ethics. What is required is a deft management of the extraneous community's expectations alongside the research goals. It is not healthy for a researcher to wriggle out of such tricky situations through false promises and outright lies.

Non-Compensation School

One of the thorny ethical issues that nearly all fieldworkers face is reciprocity. The controversy revolves around whether one should or should not return favours in the field. Fieldworkers grapple with mundane questions of: whether to return favours or not? What to give? Who to give? When to give? and how to give. These are ethical questions with hidden consequences if mishandled. Scholars supportive of returning favours argue that reciprocity is a virtue and that it is insensitive, inhuman and outright exploitation to take for granted the goodwill extended to a fieldworker by the informants. Those opposed to returning favours contend that oral literature is owned by all members of the community, therefore no person has a copyright on it. Furthermore, they aver that giving inducements promotes bribery that inadvertently encourages bias that leads to data contamination.

Seth Kotch, while sharing SOHP experiences in documenting the oral history of the American South, advised researchers at the University of Nairobi against giving inducements to respondents during fieldwork. He observed that in the American society, interviewing respondents is considered an honour to those selected. Respondents are therefore proud to have been nominated to take part in the study, and for that reason there is no compulsion to reward them. Expectation or solicitation for any form of inducement or compensation is therefore unimaginable in such a society. Kotch advised that, as much as possible, compensation, unless absolutely unavoidable, should be kept out of the fieldwork plan. The situation captured by Kotch indicates that compensation can be influenced by self esteem, attitudes and socio-economic status of the informants.

I had a similar experience when conducting fieldwork in Seoul Metropolitan Region (SMR), Korea in 2011-2012. It was not easy for respondents to accept appreciation from us, especially when it was in cash form. But when we gave out gifts, they readily took them. My Korean informants did not explicitly state why they were not willing to take gifts from us. It was obvious that coming from Africa, they assumed we are too poor to have anything to give them. They found it embarrassing to receive a token from a person from a continent under the 'burden of poverty and disease.' I remember a touching case of an old lady informant who declined to take her gift despite her poor situation. When I pleaded with her to take the token, she made sure that she bought me a gift of a higher value a week later.

Wanjiku Kabira and Ciarunji Chesaina, both authors of books on Kenyan oral literature and advocates of the 'compensation school' did not agree with Kotch's thesis. They argued that oral artists are human beings with obligations. They do not live on "honour" or "respect," they need money to participate in the cash-based economy like other members of the society. The two Kenyan scholars averred that informants regardless of whether they are oral artists or opinion leaders suspend their work during fieldwork to offer information that a researcher badly needs. The information retrieved from the individual members of the community enables the researcher to climb social ladder, get academic grades, publish books and, in some cases, get economic rewards.

Scholars with reservations against compensating informants are not confined to the developed economies like the US, Europe and parts of Asia; they are also found in Africa. Okpewho and Okogbo find similar trends in some African communities. Okpewho (1992, 357), in particular, notes that even in some African communities, "it would be considered an insult to offer money to informants and even awkward to raise the issue". Okogbo also reflecting on her fieldwork experience remembers the testimony of one of her students who was told by the group she recorded in her home town: "Even if you did not give us money at all, we are happy that you are going to tell the world about us" (18). Scholars opposed to compensation also mention methodological and ethical grounds for their position. They cite 'communal authorship' and potential for corruption as reasons for their reluctance to compensate informants. They contend that oral literature is owned by all members of the community, therefore no individual has a copyright on it. Considering the increased sensitivity to attempts to manipulate, influence or coarse community members to take part in a study against their will, the 'no-compensation school' fears that payment for data amounts to corruption and is therefore unethical as it may lead to deliberate data contamination. Among the Luo community of western Kenya, where I come from, there is a common saying that, "*Jakech iye gone nengo*" (A hungry man bargains with his stomach). It suggests that a starving informant should not be expected to be rational in bargaining with a schooled fieldworker. The deprived conditions of informants in Africa expose them to manipulation and exploitation as suggested by scholars opposed to compensation.

Self-Compensation

The 'no compensation school' has a sub-group of scholars that argues that apart from the ethical and methodological concerns, artists should not be compensated because, often times, they 'compensate themselves' abundantly in other ways. Accordingly, if some artists are poor, it is not because the society does not compensate them adequately, but rather because of their misplaced priorities and imprudent lifestyles. At the 8th ISOLA Conference in Mombasa, Kenya (July, 2010), the issue of compensation for artists was looked at closely and from varied positions. Two positions became distinct: one fronted by Russel Katchulla and the other by Godini Darah. While Katchulla supported giving compensation to artists based on ethical and economic principles, Darah, a Nigerian folklorist with decades of research in oral poetry, opposed it arguing that artists reward themselves abundantly with pleasure and therefore do not deserve another 'payment' as it would amount to 'double-payment.'

The two opposing schools ground their arguments on ethical considerations. Katchulla, echoing Chesaina and Kabira's position contends that compensation for artists should not be discretionary. The society is based on cash economy and artists are part of the capitalist society in which profit motive is the overriding factor in any enterprise, performance included. The 'compensation school' argues further that poets visit supermarkets for provisions and hospitals for health care. They also pay rent, extend assistance to needy cases and send their children to school just like other wage-earning members of the society. It is therefore only proper that they are compensated well for the services they deliver to the society. Darah, in opposing compensation for artists, observes that artists and pleasure are inseparable. They reward themselves abundantly, and as such, are well taken care of by society.

Appreciation of informants is never prioritized in qualitative research design. I remember mounting a strong argument with the university administration in 2003 on the need to include 'honoraria' for informants in our budgets for fieldwork. The

Department of Literature eventually convinced the university administration that the fact that local artists do not have the capacity to bargain over their property (traditional knowledge) is not enough reason to deny them their rightful compensation. As Madge (145) explains, oral artists are normally selected because they have above average traditional knowledge of their folklore that research institutions are interested in. Compensation becomes recognition of the value of intangible heritage preserved by these unacknowledged community archives. Payback, then functions as "an underlying principle, a state of mind, or a state of conscience" (Hawes 70). The University of Nairobi currently recognises local artists/ respondents participating in fieldwork, as experts or consultants on their own values, knowledge, skills and experiences and makes provision for a modest compensation during fieldwork. Tokens do not have to be monetary. Depending on the needs of the community and value system, acceptable gifts can be offered from tobacco to clothes. In one instance, I made my fieldwork students collect clothe donations from fellow students in the halls as tokens to the host community. It had a greater impact than money. We had three bales of good clothes that we handed over to the local Rotary Club in the research area for distribution to needy cases.

University of Nairobi students presenting donation of clothes to Rotary Club
of Maralal. *Picture by Peter Wasamba. March 2005*

Fieldwork in Conflict Zone

Conflicts similar to the clashes that Kenya has been experiencing
periodically since 1992, exposes fieldworkers to the dangers of
being targeted due to their ethnic backgrounds. Fieldworkers are
also likely to be swayed by ethnic loyalty to spy on the host
communities they study, depending on their ethnic relationships.
Surprisingly, literature that examines physical dangers to
fieldworkers operating in armed conflict environment is quite
limited. Some of the writers who have devoted time to
fieldworkers at risk are (Gill 2004), (Howell 1990) and (Kovats-
Bernat 2002). Anthropologists have suggested that
contemporary fieldwork is more dangerous than it was in the
past. The various abuses of fieldwork made by governmental

intelligence agencies in the past, may reinforce, in some quarters, the general suspicion that fieldworkers are spies of some description (Belousov, Konstantin, *et al*. 2007, 156).

Franz Boas, the father of academic anthropology in America, was one of the early scholars to expose the vulnerability of field research to unethical practices in a world embroiled in wars. In the years preceding World War I, he was outraged when he realized that anthropological field research might have been used by the US State Department as a camouflage for systematic espionage (797). He was infuriated by the discovery that a few ethnographers, trusted by host communities as non-partisan, allowed themselves to be (mis)used as spies for the United States and other friendly governments before and during the Great War. Under the heading "Scientists as Spies," Boas charged that four American anthropologists had abused their professional research positions by conducting espionage in Central America during the World War I. Boas strongly condemned their actions, arguing that they had "prostituted science by using it as a cover for their activities as spies." So disturbed was Boas that he asserted that; a scientist who uses his/her fieldwork activity as a cover for political spying forfeits the right to be classified as a scientist but a 'prostitute.'

Ironically, at the annual meeting of the American Anthropological Association (AAA), which came ten days after the publication of Boas' letter, the father of ethics in ethnographic research was disgraced and unanimously censured by the governing council. He was removed from the council and prevailed upon to resign from other national research positions for condemning researchers 'helping' their motherland in times of great peril. Boas did not name the spies he had alluded to. It was, however, later confirmed that the 'spying fieldworkers' were: Samuel Lothrop, Sylvanus Morley, Herbert Spinden and John Mason. Indeed, Mason later wrote Boas an apologetic letter explaining that he had spied out of a sense of patriotic duty to his country.

FBI documents accessed by David Price (2000), under the Freedom of Information Act confirmed Franz Boas' fears long after his death. The FBI files confirmed that the Harvard archaeologist, Samuel Lothrop, spied for Naval Intelligence, during World War I, in the Caribbean until his identity as an Agent of Naval Intelligence became known. World War II saw Lothrop back, serving in the Special Intelligence Service (SIS) in Lima, Peru, where he monitored imports, exports and political developments while pretending to be conducting archaeological investigations. In September 2007, the Pentagon, for the first time, openly deployed teams of anthropologists and social scientists to each of the 26 American combat brigades in Iraq and Afghanistan. Academicians immediately condemned the unholy alliance and called on anthropologists not to offer their services to the American forces, accused of making the world more insecure. A number of scholars have dismissed colleagues working with the military as 'mercenary anthropologists exploiting social science for political gain'. Scientists opposed to the programme fear that, whatever their intention, anthropologists who work with the military may, inadvertently cause all anthropologists to be viewed as intelligence gatherers for the military outfits that employ them (Rohde David 2009).

The concern raised by Boas is not really whether an anthropologist should spy for his or her country in times of peril. His concern is a fundamental ethical question of whether a fieldworker can hide his/her spying activities under fieldwork. Boas is not against researchers spying for their countries in times of need. In any case, it would be difficult to monitor spying activities of individuals, especially in this technological era. His position is that people are free to do what they want to do for themselves and their governments, but they should not devalue the dignity of fieldwork with activities like spying as they desecrate and endanger the profession and the remaining unblemished researchers.

Though a study has not been conducted in Kenya on the role of fieldworkers as spies for the government or opposition parties, especially during general elections, it cannot be ruled out. Academic independence together with ethical practice always take a back seat during elections as researchers support narrow ethnic agenda. In 1997, the former president Moi assembled the best team of researchers from all public universities and research institutions in the country. They were sent to their ethnic communities or rural areas neighbouring their ethnic communities to conduct 'research' on who was likely to win the hotly contested multi-party elections in Kenya. All pollsters had indicated that the incumbent, president Daniel arap Moi, was losing to opposition. It later emerged that the professors, many of them, respected names in academic community, were not engaged in any known research activity. They were monitoring the mood of the electorate in order to advice Moi and his operatives on new tactics to employ to subvert the will of the people. As a result, Moi operatives resorted to rigging since he was not going to win in an open ballot. The project raised fundamental questions in terms of how far a researcher can go in working with ethnic-driven political groups without going against research ethics. It also ignited debate on how a researcher who becomes a political party activist can be redeemed after the elections?

Ethical Dilemmas

Based on some of the challenges I've mentioned above, it is my considered view that the practical way to debate emerging issues in ethics and oral literature fieldwork is to look at the ethical dilemmas that researchers face in their practice and the decisions they take to promote research while protecting themselves and the rights of those studied. I will refer to specific cases of ethical dilemmas and the decisions taken at the time. The ethical dilemmas I discuss are both theoretical and methodological. They include obeying the law or respecting confidentiality principle, concealing information that can save lives, dealing with informants who disown their recorded testimonies and collecting data through deceit.

In the aftermath of the 2007/8 post-election violence in Kenya, I started questioning my old approach to fieldwork as an open classroom for researchers because it was based on the theory of cultural relativism. This is an intellectual stance that allows a researcher to study how and why people act as they do. This approach is premised on the fact that to prejudge the morality of people, to be concerned with how they ought to act before finding out how they do, skews research. Like ethno-methodology, the approach encourages fieldworkers to wear the community lens and empathetically partner with the community in the research process. The arguments advanced by cultural relativists are quite persuasive. But after the violence I witnessed, I'm now questioning why a fieldworker should automatically accept any or all of the practices of the people being studied as morally acceptable. Does the approach suggest that a community is always right, even if it is engaged in criminal activities like looting and burning houses of a neighbouring community? Does exposing a community's threat to neighbouring communities, a common phenomenon in Northern Kenya, amount to spying and therefore unethical? What do I do when I see harmful, illegal, or wrongful behaviour on the part of others during a study? Should I speak for anyone's interests besides my own? If so, whose interests do I advocate? (Miles and Huberman, 293).

Northern Kenya is a hardship area with pastoralists engaged in endless cattle rustling activities. With acquisition of guns, cattle rustlers have become so daring. They engage their opponents and law enforcement agents in quasi-conventional warfare. Many government officers have lost their lives in the line of duty in this region. In 2005, while conducting research among the five conflicting communities in the region, I visited a small town ravaged by armed conflict. We had a lively focused group discussion with community leaders including priests and chiefs. All the chiefs and their subjects were camping in this town as internally displaced persons due to hostilities from a neighbouring community notorious for national and cross-border cattle rustling. The discussion became animated as participants lamented lack of government support to protect them from raiders.

Within a short time, the discussion entered a delicate topic concerning the downing of a government helicopter in the area. Suddenly, one old man confessed that he and majority of the residents knew the person who committed the crime which resulted in the deaths of senior government official two years earlier. Members of the group agreed with him. I was shocked by the revelation. The senior administrator, together with other government officers accompanying him, died in a brutal way. They were pursuing cattle rustlers who had raided a neighbouring community, killed villagers and made away with several heads of animals when suspected rustlers brought down their low-flying chopper using a riffle. My dilemma in this case was: When do we go back to the law of the land and not ethical principles? Must fieldworkers be on the side of the law even if it compromises their confidentiality contract with informants? Are fieldworkers insulated by the law like lawyers and journalists who are allowed not to disclose their sources or clients? Can a researcher use the information given to him/her in the line of duty to hand over a respondent/suspect to law enforcement agencies? Is it in order for a fieldworker to hide a suspect or conceal crime witnessed during research? Where is the meeting point between researcher-respondent confidentiality and researcher's civic responsibility? I chose to respect the confidentiality contract with my informants and never reported the matter. It is not easy because you know the families of the victims are crying for justice and you are in a position to help them get it but you won't. I was traumatized for some time.

I encountered a similar dilemma in 2007. I had been commissioned by an organization to research on the relationship between armed conflict waged by a local militia and the frequency and intensity of violence against women in the community. The research had come at a time when the government had deployed the military, paramilitary and the regular police to disarm the militia members in the research location bordering a neighbouring country. The militia command responded by becoming more vicious. They were targeting armed personnel and local civilians perceived to be informers and killing them in the most brutal way. It was alleged that the leader of the militia was a former police officer with specialized commando training in Israel. When I informed my friends that I was going to the mountain for three weeks to conduct interviews on violence in the region, they thought I was crazy. But my three local research assistants assured me of security. I learnt that the greatest resource during fieldwork in a war environment is reliable assistants. They knew where fighting was, who were involved, who had been affected and what the combatants were saying about my presence in the area. On two occasions, interviews were disrupted by gun fighting between the militia and government security in broad daylight.

One of the disturbing experiences I took time to get over was of a widow who witnessed her husband being murdered by the militia, after which she was dragged to the banana plantation and rapped by nine gang members. Too damaged to walk, she crawled to safety where the government had opened up a security camp. Instead of getting medical support, she was rapped again by five security officers and left for dead. When I met her, she was sick, homeless, penniless and traumatized. The rebel leader would come out of hiding in the mountain unannounced and explain to the locals why they had to fight the government and traitors. I decided to interview him knowing too well it was dangerous to do so.

Through my trusted networks in the community, I communicated to the rebel leader that I wanted to interview him for research only. Meanwhile, intelligence officers sent from the head office in Nairobi were camping in a town neighbouring the conflict zone. I happened to stay in the same town and we were residents in the same hotel. We would meet in the evening during dinner and we would discuss general issues. They informed me they were coordinating the operation in the mountain. The following day, my contact with the rebel leader informed me that he had agreed that we could meet in a secret place for the interview. There was one condition though: If we were caught interviewing him, we were all going to die because he was armed and he was going to fight back to the last breath or bullet. I came back to my hotel in the evening confused. As usual, I met the security officers at dinner. I started debating within myself whether it was in order to conceal this vital information, especially when I had recorded testimonies of widows who had seen their husbands killed and had been raped by the militia. Then I thought about my responsibility as a family man. Would it be in order to risk my young family to interview the bandit? I decided to become selfish for once. I put my life first, my young family second, then ethical responsibility and civic duty last. I dropped the request to interview the rebel leader. I did not divulge the vital information to the security as it was not my core duty as a fieldworker. I went on with my research to the end uninterrupted but troubled at heart. At one point I thought that it would be good for fieldworkers in risky environments to have counsellors so that they do not implode from secrets bottle-up within them.

My field experiences are consistent with what other researchers have gone through in similar situations. While conducting field work among urban Africans during early 1973 du Toit found himself the confidant of a number of persons who were organizing a major strike. He was committed to presenting the social, economic and political predicament of these urban residents, and they told him about the strike well in advance of the February first red-letter day. He had information which, if shared with the administration, could have prevented property damage and danger to the lives of the strikers. He chose to remain loyal to the informants and ethics in fieldwork (du Toit, B. M., 276-7).

Apart from the scaring episodes like the three alluded to, other ethical dilemmas touch on the ownership of the research data. For instance, what happens when respondent disown their recorded testimonies at the end of the study after the report is published and disseminated? The Kenya Oral Literature Association (KOLA) in partnership with Panos London and Ford Foundation conducted an oral testimonies project in five districts in Kenya between 1996 and 2001 (Masinjila, M and O Okombo

1998). One of the research sites was Mt. Elgon District. The study took place after the 1992 ethnic conflict in the area which saw members of communities considered outsiders evicted from their land. The objective of the study was to capture local people's perceptions of development from their own perspectives.

The project was part of peace building process to bring warring communities together. Further, the project aimed at giving local people, previously ignored by policy makers, voice to articulate their ideas of development based on their memory of what had worked or not worked for them. I was a research assistant in the project. The project entailed recording life histories in local languages on tapes, conducting transcription, translation, analysis, and publishing the testimonies into a book. The first book published in 2000 was based on personal life histories of respondents from Mt. Elgon. During the study, one respondent who was a high school teacher was highly critical of the government of President Moi. He was categorical that Moi had marginalised the Sabaots, his ethnic community. He gave his consent for the interview to be published. By the time the book entitled, *Voices from the Mountain: Personal Life Histories from Mt. Elgon* came out in 2000, the respondent had changed his political beliefs and was now an ardent supporter of President Moi. The book was launched in Mt. Elgon and the community was quite happy, especially those who told their stories. By this time, I had become the project coordinator.

After a few days, the respondent called to tell me that after reading his published testimony and also considering the political situation, he had changed his mind about everything he said about Moi. He no longer subscribed to the views expressed in the book and wanted his story expunged from all copies printed. He also demanded that the book be withdrawn from circulation because it endangered not only his job as a civil servant but also his life, since Moi was known to use secret police against his opponents. My big worry regarding the case was: How do you deal with a respondent who disowns his/her testimony after the data has been analyzed and published into a book? Is it ethical to publish controversial statements made by a respondent, even if he/she is agreeable to the publication? Is it acceptable to destroy valuable data after analysis when the respondent comes back to claim his/her life is in danger? Who owns the right to an oral testimony collected by a researcher and published by the client who commissioned the study? How far can fieldworkers go in exercising judgment in terms of what to include and what to leave out when publishing personal testimonies? The board of Kola decided to exclude the interview in the subsequent publications.

Closely related to disowning a published testimony is the case of informants granting interviews but with strict caveats that renders them useless as data in the foreseeable future. This happens when an informant grants an interview but places a condition that the content of the interview should not be made public for a given period of time or until he/she dies? This is likely to happen where the interviewee feels the publication is likely to injure his/her reputation or expose him/her to criminal prosecution. For instance, a hardcore criminal who has murdered several people, a public figure afflicted with a chronic condition or a politician who is gay in a conservative society would not want the truth about them to be published when they are still alive. The researcher or the institution must respect this request and wait for the death of the respondent. Depending on his age and way of life, this can take quite long. It is also unethical to wish your informant death so that you can use the interview data. There is another catch that a researcher may not be aware of others mentioned adversely in such interviews.

In one of the states in the US, a senior politician gave an interview about his life in which he confessed to be gay. The secret was not known to the public. He then gave instruction that his interview should not be published until he dies. The institution waited until the interviewee died. When the tape was processed for publication, researchers noticed that the interviewee had implicated several high-ranking persons in the community as being gay. The people implicated were still alive. These people did not know that their late friend had exposed them in his testimony as being gay. Was the researcher going to publish the testimony knowing too well that the publication would injure the reputation of people who were still alive? The publication could certainly open a floodgate of defamation suits. The best decision in this particular case was to keep the testimony sealed until all the persons adversely mentioned are dead. The institution consequently decided not to publish the interview at all. Is it therefore necessary to collect information that you are not likely to use for years to come?

Ethics and Creative Deception

I mentioned risky fieldwork at the beginning. Fieldworkers face ethical challenges in dealing with unusual informants. These vary from drug peddlers, arms traffickers, prostitution rings, assassination squads, medicine-men and wizards. How does a researcher employ ethical standards on an unpredictable research landscape? Is deception allowed in extreme cases? Peter Amuka is one of the seasoned oral literature researchers in Kenya. In one of the workshops, he shared his experience about a collaborative research he conducted with a Japanese scholar in the 70s. The visiting scholar wanted to understand the science of night-running (wizardry) among Africans. Amuka knew a number of local wizards in Matagara village near Rongo town in South Nyanza of Western Kenya. He led the researcher to the notorious night-runner's village. Unfortunately, this kind of data could only be collected at night when the night wizard leaves for 'exercise' as the activity is politely called by villagers. Amuka and his researcher would stealthily take positions behind the man's house on selected nights to document his behaviour with the hope that he would come out for them to observe his theatrics and possibly interview him. Unfortunately, each night they went to 'collect data', the prospective informant seemed to sense their presence and would not come out to perform nocturnal running. Getting tired of the cold nights and mosquito bites, Amuka advised the lead researcher to intoxicate the night-runner in the evening with the local brew called *changaa*. Amuka hoped that under the influence of alcohol, the wizard would most likely go night-running without thinking about being observed.

The two successfully invited the informant for a 'friendly drink' one evening. They bought a 5L jerican of liquor and went to a secluded place under a tree to drink undisturbed. The Japanese researcher found the alcohol quite enjoyable and started drinking alongside the prospective informant as part of the rapport creation. Amuka, being a tee-tola, was entertaining them with humorous stories. According to Amuka, he woke up, late in the night and found the lead researcher drunk and deep asleep and the informant nowhere to be seen. The night-runner had disappeared with the jerican of *changaa*. The research ended without getting primary data on night-running.

Using the Amuka case as an example, we can ask whether deception of participants in research is acceptable. Should fieldworkers always tell the truth? Should we encourage others to behave in ways they may not otherwise? Is it acceptable to break the law to get vital data? Is it acceptable to violate privacy of others in the process of research? Are there situations when informed consent may never be given and therefore should not be sought or respected? These dilemmas confirm that fieldworkers do not cease being human beings when they embark on research. "Most fieldworkers are unlikely to lie, cheat, or steal in the course of their work. But broken promises are not unknown. And some researchers have reported deceiving respondents about the true nature of the inquiry" (Miles and Huberman, 292). Cassell however thinks that lying cannot be avoided in human interactions. "Fieldwork, like friendship, requires a number of social lies to keep interaction flowing fairly smoothly.... Such "deceit" is probably necessary in fieldwork and in social life (Cassell, J, 35). There is always a delicate balance in deciding on what is ethical and what is not. It is not possible to have one response. It all depends on the situation.

As a fieldworker with contacts in multiple Kenyan communities, I'm well aware that the ethical dilemmas mentioned are not the only ones ethnographers are likely to encounter in a conflicted society. What is apparent, however, is that fieldwork, like other ethnographic studies, is an ethical calling. The debate should encourage researchers to reflect on the challenges they face in the course of research and strategies they've employed to address them. Oral literature scholars should formulate a code of ethics to guide fieldworkers in order to uphold high levels of professionalism in the field. Such code of ethics should not only meet the international standards but also encourage continuous training in and ongoing access to education programs in ethics. In that way, fieldworkers will not fear navigating the complex terrains created by conflicting ethnic communities or countries. By citing these cases I am not presenting myself as the epitome of ethical probity in the field. I am not perfect. I have also made mistakes in the field. But I was taught that in teaching you start with the positive examples and forget about the errors of judgment that might have occurred.

Finally, good practice requires that researchers ensure they get permission to use the data they collect from informants. Fieldworkers should always ask oral artists for permission to share the recorded information with other people through media. Traditionally, it is expected that permission should be given in writing, using a prepared document called a "release form". This is particularly important if the documentary materials being created will be housed in a public archive or used in a public venue such as online presentations, print publications, documentary films, or television. "Release Form" may be brief and clear as the one attached below:

Release Form A

Informant's Name_____

Address_____

Phone Number_____

1. I agree that the transcripts, tapes and pictures of the interview(s) given by me on the following dates _____ should be made available by_____ (sponsoring institution) to members and researchers.

2. I agree that the university/research institute may publish or cause to be published all or part of the interview transcripts, pictures and tapes.

3. The information should only be used to further the cause of scholarship

    Informant's Signature _____

    Date_____

    Witness Name _____

    Signature_____

    Date _____

In some cases, the release form can be detailed as the one below:

Release Form B

I, _____, am a participant in the
_____project, (hereinafter "project").
I understand that the purpose of the project is to collect audio
and video-tapes and selected related documentary materials
(such as photographs and manuscripts) that may be deposited in
the permanent collections of _____.
The deposited documentary materials may be used for scholarly,
educational, and other purposes. I understand that the
university/research institution plans to retain the product of my
participation as part of its permanent collection and that the
materials may be used for exhibition, publication, presentation
on the World Wide Web and successor technologies, and for
promotion of the institution and its activities in any medium.

I hereby grant to _____ ownership
of the physical property delivered to the institution and the right
to use the property that is the product of my participation (for
example, my interview, performance, photographs, and written
materials) as stated above. By giving permission, I understand
that I do not give up any copyright or performance rights that I
may hold.

I also grant to _____ my absolute
and irrevocable consent for any photograph(s) provided by me or
taken of me in the course of my participation in the project to be
used, published, and copied by _____
and its assignees in any medium.

I agree that _____ may use my
name, video or photographic image or likeness, statements,

performance, and voice reproduction, or other sound effects without further approval on my part.

ACCEPTED AND AGREED

Signature _____Date_____

Printed name_____

Address_____

_____

Postal Code_____

Telephone (fixed line)_____

Telephone (Mobile line)_____

Email _____

WITNESSED BY

Signature _____Date_____

Printed name_____

Address_____

_____

Postal Code_____

Telephone (fixed line)_____

Telephone (Mobile line) _____

Email _____

Fieldworkers are free to use the release form that they find applicable. For example, I've learned that taking a detailed release form to illiterate informants smells of mischief since some of the words in English may not have their equivalents in the local lingo. Paul Thomson argues that 'an insistence on a formal transfer of legal rights through explicit, written consent may not only worry an informant, but will actually reduce proper protection of informants against exploitation by researchers or the sponsoring institutions (Thomson Paul, 225). The current thinking finds the use of 'release form' an abuse of trust between the artist and the researcher. A fieldworker cannot walk into a home, build trust and friendships with trusting members of the home, ask for and get performances (mostly offered for free) and then finally ambush the artist with a legally binding document for signature. The best approach is to get informed consent orally, and where possible record the same on audio or videotape. If you have to haggle over the signing of release form, postpone it to the end of the performance because it may dampen the mood of the artist and audience.

Other Fieldwork Challenges

Ethical dilemmas are not the only challenges fieldworkers encounter in the field. There are also other general challenges that researchers deal with on a regular basis depending on the type of research and the location. Young researchers have a tendency of treating challenges as insurmountable obstacles to research. In deed, you will notice on reading the reports of first-time researchers that they are thin on data analysis and quite generous in giving graphic details of how they encountered numerous difficulties that impeded their work. I always advice my students to transform fieldwork challenges into opportunities for displaying their resilience. Approaching challenges as research road-blocks is defeatist and unscholarly. In fact, fieldwork challenges bring out the best in a researcher since one ends up making intelligent decisions that one never thought he/she could make.

There can be no fieldwork without challenges. In our discussion of methodology in oral literature research, we noted that even though we come up with beautiful designs for fieldwork, the actual methodology is designed by circumstances prevailing in the field. One of the factors that compel a researcher to modify methodology is the challenges that pop-up during fieldwork. Sampson and Thomas (2003) concede that the risks faced by fieldworkers like health and safety issues in unfamiliar settings are frequently under-emphasized and underreported in both written and verbal accounts of fieldwork (189). Whenever researchers discuss risks, there is a tendency to sentimentalize the hardships experienced, which reduces them to scapegoats for personal inadequacies in the field. In addition, it reveals their lack of preparedness in dealing with risks. Inability to explain clearly the challenges encountered during fieldwork leaves a gap in the research process, which denies the reader opportunity to understand the context in which some of the claims made were arrived at. This explains why there is 'increasing interest in the risks that researchers must negotiate in the course of their work' (Treweek and Linkogle, 8). Even when a researcher is operating in a familiar environment, there is no guarantee that the study will be free from risks. Risk does occur any time and unexpectedly.

Reflections on challenges and dilemmas in unfamiliar domains are an inevitable part of the research process. The researcher enquires about potential danger in an attempt to understand his/her immediate social world in order to navigate around its contours and rough edges (Linkogle 2000, 132). As Linkogle has noted, the researcher is empowered and better protected against danger with this knowledge. This kind of probing can make researchers recognize a risk when they see one. There is the risk of being misunderstood and discredited later, especially, if the fieldworker is a stranger to the community. Due to the upsurge in nationalism, communities are too sensitive when studying research reports done by 'outsiders' on their way of life. It may take only one malicious person to question your integrity and provoke the whole community to discredit and disown the entire work. At times, this rebellion comes years after the fieldworker has left the research site. Through the process of historical revisionism, the well-motivated, honest, humane, and compassionate involvement of researchers with folk artists is "condemned self-righteously by later generations as patronizing, exploitative, and corrupt" (Proschan F 149).

Stuck in the mud, Oral Literature fieldworkers push the van near Maralal, Kenya 2004. *Picture by Peter Wasamba*

The table below catalogues some of the challenges that fellow fieldworkers and I have encountered in various research encounters, and how we addressed them. The list is not exhaustive. You are encouraged to reflect on your fieldwork trail and extend the list further.

Table 2: Fieldwork Challenges and Strategies

Challenges Students Anticipate	Strategies
Language barrier	• Get a good local assistant • Record the performances accurately • Plan to spend more time in the field • Learn the local language
Time constraints	• Design a research project that fits within the time available • Set aside a few extra days just in case there is need to extend the study • Conduct fieldwork in phases • Have a clear methodology to reduce time wastage • Adhere to the research schedule as much as possible • Work over-time to make up for time lost
Bad weather	• Know weather conditions in advance • Prepare adequately for bad weather
Unreliable field assistants	• Develop a criteria for selecting field assistants • Recruit local assistants transparently • Consult opinion leaders extensively to vet local assistants shortlisted • Have alternate local assistants just in case you decide to drop some • Ensure there is no nepotism in the

	recruitment
	• Induct local assistants into your fieldwork project
	• Discuss issues of payments and ethics exhaustively
	• Assign local assistants clear tasks
	• Compensate them for their support adequately and in time
	• Develop a lasting relationship beyond research project
Hostility from the community	• Introduce yourself using accepted channels
	• Participate in open community activities
	• Make friends with the local people
	• Let the community know what you are doing
	• Appreciate their culture genuinely
	• Maintain non-partisanship
	• Do not provoke the community
	• Use people respected as local assistants
Illness in the field	• Identify medical facilities close to the research site
	• Be knowledgeable in First aid
	• Have a well stocked First Aid kit with you
	• Take preventive drugs before the journey
	• Avoid risky behaviour in the field
	• Use herbal medicine approved by local experts

	• Be accessible to a health facility
Bad terrain	• Know the terrain well before the exercise
	• Prepare accordingly to cover the terrain
	• Use appropriate and reliable local means of transport
	• Allocate adequate time for movements
Equipment failure	• Assemble all the machines and their accessories in good time
	• Make sure all the machines are serviceable
	• Know how to operate the equipment
	• Have a back up equipment, just in case one fails
	• Work in teams
Uncooperative artists/ respondents	• Use resourceful local assistants
	• Be thorough in rapport creation
	• Remain patient and diplomatic
	• Have culturally acceptable incentives
	• Have reserve informants for fallback
Culture shock	• Gather a lot of information about the community you are visiting before the actual field visit
	• Expect the unexpected
	• Be ready to adjust accordingly
Very long narratives	• Remain patient and diplomatic
	• Agree on the average time limit before the performance begins
	• Never walk out on an informant

	• Never interfere with an artist/respondent in the middle of a performance • Have adequate tapes and batteries
Transport to and within the field	• Get a reliable means of transport • Have a disciplined transport crew • Prepare for alternative means of transport • Ensure that your shoes and clothes are comfortable for walking
Political environment	• Maintain political neutrality in the field • Avoid fieldwork during political campaigns and elections • Never use local politicians or their close relatives as your guides or research assistants
Insecurity	• Know the geography of the fieldwork site well • Do a thorough investigation to know the local security situation • Involve local leaders and provincial administration in your activity • Do not expose yourself too much
Financial constraints	• Ensure you have enough money to last you the research days • Keep your money safely and avoid moving around with large amounts • Carry surplus in case of emergency • Stick to your budget to avoid running bankrupt too soon

	• Never borrow money from the community members
Inducements for artists	• Explain to artists that you are a researcher
	• Have a modest gift for artists
	• Do not create the impression that you have a lot of money to give away
	• Do not steal from artists by denying them inducements set aside for them
Difficult local administrators	• Have all the papers allowing you to do research
	• Get necessary authorization before going to the field
	• Pay a courtesy call on the local administrator (DC, DO etc)
	• Learn from the administrator the dos and don'ts in the community
	• Be law abiding
	• Avoid bad company

In this last section, we have elucidated the need for preparedness and balanced state of mind in fieldwork. Without sounding alarmist, we have demonstrated that nothing should be taken for granted in the field. Even mundane issues like compensation for respondents can torpedo research in its infancy. A fieldworker interacts with various stake holders, governmental agencies and individuals including colleagues, students, sponsors, local administration, informants and local assistants in the host communities. An astute fieldworker must know how to accommodate the delicate interests of various stakeholders in a project so that their diverse energies are harnessed for the good of the community, the discipline and the researcher. It is apparent that depending on the issues at hand, dealing with each of these groups exposes a fieldworker to various ethical dilemmas and other related fieldwork challenges. It is important that a fieldworker anticipates some of these issues so that remedial measures are contemplated before they occur. We have also demonstrated that in normal circumstances, various forms of challenges are expected. But there are some challenges that are uniquely specific to certain studies. It is therefore not possible to anticipate all challenges one is likely to encounter in the field. Nevertheless, it is important that a researcher remains alert to dangers in the field to avoid personal harm to herself or other people involved in the study.

Bibliography

Abrams, Lynn. (2010). *Oral History Theory*. Routledge, London and New York.

Adagala, K and Wanjiku M. Kabira. Eds. (1985). *Kenyan Oral Narratives: A Selection*. Nairobi: Heinemann Kenya.

Aguilar, J. L. (1981). "Insider research: An ethnography of a debate." In D. A. Messerschmidt (Ed.), *Anthropologists at home in North America*. London: Cambridge University Press.

Akeroyd, Anne. (1984). "Ethics in Relation to Informants: The Profession and Governments." In *Ethnographic Research: A Guide to General Conduct*. Roy F. Ellen, ed. Pp. 133-154. London: Academic Press.

Alcoff Linda. (1995). "The Problem of Speaking for Others. Who can Speak? *Authority and Critical Identity*. Ed. Judith Roof and Robin Wiegman. Urbana: University of Illinois Press, pp 97 - 119.

Anyumba, H. O. (1964). *Nyatiti Lament Songs*. Paris: East Africa Past and Present. *Presence Africaine*.

Baron, R & Nick Spitzer. (2007). *Public Folklore*, (eds), Jackson: University Press of Mississippi. Jackson

Barthes, Roland. (1975). 'An Introduction to the structural analysis of narrative', *New Literary History* 6: 237 – 72.

Bascom, W. R. (1955). 'Verbal Art', *Journal of American Folklore* 68: 245 – 52),

Belsey, Catherine. (1980) *Critical Practice*, Routledge. Methuen

Bong A. S. (2002). "Debunking Myths in Qualitative Data Analysis in FQS" - Forum Qualitative Sozialforschung / Forum: Qualitative Social Research (ISSN 1438-5627) Volume 3, No. 2 – May 2002. Full paper found at *http://www.qualitative-research.net/fqs-texte/2-02/2-02bong-e.htm*

Bolter, Jay David. (1991).*Writing Space: The Computer, Hypertext and the History of Writing*. Hillsdale, NJ: Lawrence Erlbaum.

Botkin, B. A. (1953). "Applied Folklore: Creating Understanding through Folklore." Southern Folklore Quarterly 17: 199 – 206.

Brooke Robert and Charlotte Hogg. (2004). "Open to Change: Ethos, Identification and Critical Ethnography in Composition Studies". *Ethnography Unbound: From Post-modern theory Shock to Critical Praxis*. Ed. Stephen G Brown and Sidney I. Dobrin. Albany: State University of New York Press.

Bradbury, Malcolm. "What was Post-Modernism? The Arts in and after the Cold War": *International Affairs (Royal Institute of International Affairs* (1944), Vol. 71, No. 4, Special RIIA 75th Anniversary Issue (Oct., 1995), pp. 763-774

Brockmeier, J. and R. Harre. (2001) "Narrative: Problems and Promises of an Alternative Paradigm" in J. Brockmeier and D. Carbough (eds) *Narrative and Identity: Studies in Autobiography, Self and Culture*. Amsterdam, pp 39-58. John Benjamins.

Brown, S. G & Sidney I. Dobrin. (2004) *Ethnography Unbound: From Theory Shock to Critical Praxis*. Albany: State University of New York Press.

Chadwick H. M. and N. K. (1932 – 40). *The Growth of Literature, 3 Vols,* Cambridge: Cambridge University Press.

Chesaina, Ciarunji, (1996) *Oral Literature of the Embu and Mbeere.* Nairobi: East African Educational Publishers.

Chiseri-Strater Elizabeth & Bonnie Stone Sunstein. (1997)*Field Working: Reading and Writing Research.* Boston: Bedford/St. Martin's. Field Working Online *http://www.fieldworking.com.*

Celarent, Barbara. *"Facing Mount Kenya* by Jomo Kenyatta." *American Journal of Sociology,* The University of Chicago Press, Vol. 116, No. 2 (September 2010), pp. 722-728 *http://www.jstor.org/stable/10.1086/658069*

Clifford, James. (1990c). "Notes on (Field) notes." In Roger Sanjek, ed. *Fieldnotes: The Making of Anthropology,* 47-70. Ithaca, NY.: Cornell University Press.

Clough, P and Cathy Nutbrown. (2002). A Student's Guide to Methodology. London: SAGE.

Cassell, Joan. "Ethical Principles for Conducting Fieldwork." *American Anthropologist, New Series,* Vol. 82, No. 1 (Mar., 1980), pp. 28-41: Blackwell Publishing on behalf of the American Anthropological Association. Stable URL: *http://www.jstor.org/stable/676126*

Dara, Godini. (2005). *Battles of Songs: Udje Tradition of the Urhobo.* Lagos: Malthouse Press Limited.

Drisko, J. W. (1998). Using Qualitative Data Analysis Software. *Computers in Human Services* 15 (1): 1–19.

Denzin, N.K and Lincoln, Y.S. (eds) (2000) *Handbook of Qualitative Research* (2nd edn). Thousand Oaks: Sage.

du Toit, Brian M. "Ethics, Informed Consent, and Fieldwork". *Journal of Anthropological Research*, Vol. 36, No. 3 (Autumn, 1980), pp. 274-286: University of New Mexico. Stable URL: *http://www.jstor.org/stable/3629524*

Eagleton, Terry. (1987). *Literary Theory*. Minneapolis: University of Minnesota Press.

Ellen, R. F. (ed.) (1984). *Ethnographic Research: A Guide to General Conduct*, ASDA Research Methods in Social Anthropology, 1, London: Academic Press.

Fabian, J. (1991). Dilemmas in critical anthropology. In L. Nencel and P. Pels (eds). *Constructing Knowledge: authority and critique in social science*. London: Sage. pp. 180—202.

Finnegan, Ruth. (1970). *Oral Literature in Africa*. Oxford: The Clarendon Press.

_____. (1992). *Oral traditions and the Verbal Arts*. New York: Rutledge.

Fludernik, Monika (2013). "Conversational Narration – Oral Narration," Paragraph 1 – 32. In: Hühn, Peter et al. (eds.): the living handbook of narratology. Hamburg: Hamburg University Press.

Fish, Stanley. (1989). *Doing What Comes Naturally: Change, Rhetoric, and the Practice of Theory in Literary and Legal Studies*(pg 341). Durham: Duke University Press.

Frankfort-Nachmias, Chava and David Nachmias. (1996).*Research Methods in the Social Sciences*. London: Arnold.

Freire Paulo. (1971). *Ladoc Keyhole Series, A Publication of Division of Latin America*. Washington: VSEC.

Gay E. David. (2000). "Inventing the Text: A Critique of Folklore Editing. *Folklore Vol.* 14: Eds. Mare Koiva and Andres kuperjanov. Tarta, 97 – 117.

Georges, Robert. (1980) Towards a resolution of the text/context controversy. *Western Folklore* 39. 34 – 40.

Glaser, Barney G. (2002). "Conceptualization: On Theory and Theorizing Using Grounded Theory". *International Journal of Qualitative Methods* 1 (2), Pp 1- 31

Gokah, Theophilus. (2006). "The Naïve Researcher: Doing Social Research in Africa". *Int. J. Social Research Methodology Vol. 9, No. 1, February 2006, pp. 61–73.*

Goldstein, K. S. (1964). *A Guide to Field Workers in Folklore*, Hatboro: Folklore Associates Inc. and London: Herbert Jenkins.

Good Anthony (1992). In editor's Forward to Ruth Finnegan. *Oral traditions and the Verbal Arts.* New York: Routlege.

Gordon K Walter (1968). *Literature in critical Perspectives.* New Jersey: Prentice-Hall Inc.

Grele, Ron. (1991). *Envelopes of Sound. The Art of Oral History,* New York: Precedent.

Grele, R. (1995). "History and the Languages of History in the Oral History Interview: who Answers Whose Questions and Why?" in E.M. McMahan and K.L. Rogers (eds) *Interactive Oral History Interviewing.* Hove: pp. 1 – 18. Lawrence Erlbaum Associates.

Goffman, Erving. (1989). "On Fieldwork". *Journal of Contemporary Ethnography* 18: 123 – 32.

Goldstein, K. S. (1964). *A Guide to Field Workers in Folklore,* Hatboro: Folklore Associates Inc. and London: Herbert Jenkins.

Gordon K Walter. (1968). *Literature in critical Perspectives*. New Jersey: Prentice-Hall Inc.

Horner Bruce. (2004) "Critical Ethnography, Ethics and Work: rearticulating labour." *Ethnography Unbound: From Post-modern theory Shock to Critical Praxis*. Ed. Stephen. Albany: State University of New York Press.

Hawes, B. Lomax. (2007). "Happy Birthday, Dear American Folklore Society: Reflection on the Work and Mission of Folklorists." In Baron, R & Nick Spitzer. *Public Folklore*, (eds), Jackson: University Press of Mississippi.

Hammersley, M., & Atkinson, P. (1995). *Ethnography: Principles in Practice*. London: Tavistock.

Hesford, Walter. (1992). "Overt Appropriation." *College English* 54.4: 406-17.

Honig, H. (1997). Positions, Power and Practice: Functionalist Approaches and Translation Quality Assessment. *Current Issues in Language and Society*, 4(1).

Hornby, A. S. (1990).*Oxford Advanced Learner's Dictionary of Current English*. 4th ed. London: Oxford University Press.

Horner Bruce. (2004). "Critical Ethnography, Ethics and Work: rearticulating Labour." *Ethnography Unbound: From Post-modern theory Shock to Critical Praxis*. Ed. Stephen G Brown and Sidney I. Dobrin. Albany: State University of New York Press.

Husserl, Edmund. (1931). *Ideas: General Introduction to Pure Phenomenology*. Boyce W. R. Gibson, trans. New York: Humanities Press.

Hymes Dell. (1977). *Foundations in Socio-linguistics: An Ethnographic Approach*. London: Tavistock Publications Limited.

Janheinz, Jahn. (1968). *Neo-African Literature: A History of Black Writing*, New York: Grove Press Inc.

Jones, Stephen S. (1979a). "Slouching towards ethnography: The text/context controversy considered." *Western Folklore* 38. 42 – 47.

_____. (1979b). "Dogmatism in the contextual revolution." *Western Folklore* 38. 52 – 57.

Jørgensen, Marianne and Louise Phillips. (2002). *Discourse Analysis as Theory and Method*. London: SAGE Publications.

Karpf, A. (2006). *The Human Voice: The story of a Remarkable Talent*. London, p. 4. Bloomsbury Publishing PLC.

Kaschulla, R. H and Andre Mostert. (2009). "Analyzing, Digitizing and Technologizing the Oral Word: The Case of Bongani Sitole." In *Journal of African Cultural Studies*. Vol. 21 No. 2 Dec. pp. 159 – 176.

_____. (Ed) (2001). *African Oral Literature: Functions in Contemporary Contexts*, Cape Town: New Africa Books.

_____. (1999) "Imbongi and Griot: Toward a Comparative Analysis of Oral Poetics in Southern and West Africa": *Journal of African Cultural Studies*, Vol. 12, No. 1 (Jun., 1999), pp. 55-76 Published by: Taylor & Francis, Ltd. Stable URL: *http://www.jstor.org/stable/1771848*

Kidane Sahlu. (2002). *Borana Folktales: A Contextual Study*. London: HAAN.

Kipury, Naomi. (1983). *Oral Literature of the Maasai*. Nairobi: Heinemann Educational Books.

Kirk, Jerome & Miller, Marc L. (1986). *Reliability and Validity in Qualitative Research*. London: Sage.

Kirsh, Gesa E. and Joy S. Ritchie. (1995). "Beyond the Personal: Theorizing a Politics of Location in Composition Research." *College Composition and Communication* 46: 7 – 29.

Kornblum William. (1974). *Blue-Collar Community*. Chicago: Chicago University Press.

Kothari, C.R (1990). *Research methodology: Methods and Techniques*. 2 ed., New Delhi: Vishwaprakashan.

Kvale, S. 1996. *Interviews: An introduction to qualitative research interviewing*. Thousand Oaks, CA: Sage.

Lastrucci L. Carlos. (1967). *The Scientific Approach: Basic Principles of the Scientific Method*. Cambridge: Mass.: Schenkman Publishing Co., Inc.

Lathem, Laura, (2005). "Bringing Old and Young People Together: an Interview Project". In Della Pollock. Ed. *Remembering: Oral History Performance*. New York: Palgrave Macmillan, pp. 67 – 84.

Lejeune, P. (1989). *On Autobiography*. Minneapolis, Minn., pp 131-2. University of Minnesota Press.

Limon, Jose and Mary J. Young. (1986). Frontiers, settlements, and developments in folklore studies. *Annual Review of Anthropology* 15: 437-460.

Lincoln, Bruce. (1991). *Death, War and Sacrifice: Studies in ideology and practice*, University of Chicago Press. Chicago.

Linde, C. (1993). *Life Stories: The Creation of Coherence.* New York: Oxford University Press.

Linkogle, S. (2000). Danger in a crowd. In G. L. Treweek & S. Linkogle (Eds.), *Danger in the field: Risk and ethics in social research,* pp. 132–146. London: Routledge.

Liyong, Taban. (1972). *Popular Culture in East Africa.* Nairobi: East African Literature Bureau.

_____. (1990)*Another Last Word.* Nairobi: Heinemann Kenya.

Long, N. and Villarreal M. (1994). 'The Interweaving of Knowledge and Power in Development Interfaces'. In Scoones I. and Thompson, J. (eds.). *Beyond Farmers First: Rural People's Knowledge, Agricultural Research and Extension Practice.* London: IT Publications.

Lord, Albert B. (1960).*The Singer of Tales.* Cambridge, Massachusetts: Havard University Press.

Madison, D. Soyini. (1998). "Performance, Personal Narratives, and the Politics of Possibility. *The Future of Performance Studies: Visions and Revisions.* Ed. Sheron J. dailey. Annandale, VA: National Communication Association, pp. 276 – 286.

Madge J. (1975). *The Tools of Social Science.* 2nd Impression Longman. London

Manilerd C. (1985). "The Why of Preservation of Cultural Heritage". *Thai Cultural Newsletter.* 3: 4

Malinowsky, Branislaw. (1922, 1961). *Argonauts of the Western Pacific.* London: Routledge and Kegan Paul.

Masinjila, M and Okoth Okombo. (1997). *Voices from the Mountain: Personal Life Histories from Mt. Elgon.* Nairobi: Kenya Oral Literature Association (KOLA).

Masinjila Masheti. (1992). "The Genesis of Theory: The Case for Kenyan Oral Literature". In *Reflections on Theories and Methods in Oral Literature.* (Eds) Okoth Okombo and J Nandwa. Nairobi: KOLA.

Marvin, Harris. (1979).*Cultural Materialism: The Struggle for a Science of Culture.* New York: Random House.

McGrane, Bernard. (1989). *Beyond Anthropology: Society and the Other,* Columbia UP. New York.

Meister, Jan Christoph (2013) "Narratology," Paragraph 1 – 80. In: Hühn, Peter et al. (eds.): *the living handbook of narratology.* Hamburg: Hamburg University Press.

Mishler, Elliot G. (1979). "Meaning in Context: Is There Any Other Kind?" *Harvard Education Review* 49: 1 – 9.

Mlama, P. (1995). Oral art and contemporary cultural nationalism. In Furniss & Gunner (1995), *Power, Marginality and African Oral Literature.* pp. 23-34.

Maykut, Pamela & Richard Morehouse (1994). *Beginning Qualitative Research: A Philosophic and Practical Guide.* London and Washington, DC: Falmer Press.

Mazrui, Ali. (2003). "Towards Re-Africanizing African Universities: Who Killed Intellectualism in the Post Colonial Era?" *Alternatives: Turkish Journal of International Relations,* Vol.2, No.3&4, Fall &Winter.

Messerschmidt, D. A. (Ed.) (1981). *Anthropologists at home in North America*. London: Cambridge University Press.

Muana, Patrick. Kagbeni. (1998). "Beyond Frontiers: A Review of Analytical Paradigms in Folklore Studies. Journal *of African Cultural Studies*, Vol. 11, No. 1: Taylor & Francis, Ltd., pp. 39-58.

Mulokozi, M. (1983) "The Nanga Bards of Tanzania: Are They Epic Artists?" *Research in African Literatures*, Vol. 14, No. 3, Special Issue on Epic and Panegyric Poetry in Africa (Autumn, 1983), pp. 283-311Published by: Indiana University Press Stable URL: *http://www.jstor.org/stable/3819155*

Mwangi Rose. (1976). *Kikuyu Folktales*. Nairobi: East African Literature Bureau.

Nandwa Jane and A, Bukenya. (1983). *African Oral Literature for Schools*. Nairobi: Longman Kenya.

Natanson, Maurice. (1970). "Alfred Schutz on Social Reality and Social Science". In Maurice Natanson, ed., *Phenomenology and Social Reality*. The Hague: Nijhoff

Neustadt, Kathy. (1994). The folkloristics of licking. *Journal of American Folklore* 107:181-196.

Ngara, E (1982). *Stylistic Criticism of the African Novel*. London: Heinemann

Ngugi wa Thiong'o. (1981). *Decolonising the Mind: The Politics of Language in African Literature*, Nairobi: East African Educational Publishers.

_____. (1993). *Moving the Centre: The Struggle for Cultural Freedoms.* London: James Currey; Nairobi: East African Educational Publishers; Portsmouth, NH: Heinemann.

Njoroge Ngugi. (1978). "African Oral Literature: Fighting Literature" in *Teaching of African Literature in Schools.* Vol 1. (Eds) Gachukia Eddah and S, K Akivaga. Nairobi: Kenya Literature Bureau.

Nukunya, G. K. (1969). *Kingship and marriage among the Anlo Ewe.* New York: Humanities Press.

Okombo, Okoth (1992). "The Place of Ethnomethdology in the Study of Oral Literature." In *Reflections on Theories and Methods in Oral Literature.* (Eds) Okoth Okombo and J Nandwa. Nairobi: Kenya Oral Literature Association.

Okot p'Bitek. (1966). *Song of Lawino.* Nairobi: Heinemann,

_____. *Song of Ocol,* Nairobi: Heinemann, 1967.

Okpewho, Isidore. (1992). *African Oral Literature: Backgrounds, Character and Continuity.* Bloomington and Indianapolis: Indiana University Press.

Okogbo, M. M. (1988). "The Glory of the Game: A Study of Isiko, The Hunters' Performance in Auchi." B.A Honors essay, Department of English, University of Ibadan.

Ogot B, A. (2003). *My Footprints on the Sands of Time: An Autobiography.* Oxford: Trafford.

Ong, Walter J. (1982). *Orality and Literacy: The technologizing of the word.* London: Routledge.

Patton, M. Q. (2002). *Qualitative research and evaluation methods.* 3d ed. Thousand Oaks, CA: Sage.

Perks, Robert & Alistar Thomson. Eds. (2009). *The Oral History Reader.* 2 Edition. New York, Routledge.

Phillips, H. P. (1960). Problems of translation and meaning in field work. In R. N. Adams and J. J. Preiss (eds) *Human Organisation Research: Field Relations and Techniques.* Homewood, ILL: Dorsey Press Inc.

Poland, B., and A. Pederson. (1998). Reading between the lines: Interpreting silences in qualitative research. *Qualitative Inquiry* 4:293–312. *(The paper is published online)*

Pollock, Della. Ed. (2005). *Remembering: Oral History Performance.* New York: Palgrave Macmillan.

Portelli, A. (1991). "What Makes Oral History Different?" in A, Portelli, *The Death of Luigi Trastulli and Other Stories: Form and Meaning in Oral History.* New York, pp 45 – 58. State University of New York Press.

Portelli, A. (2004). "Oral History as Genre" in Chamberlain, M. and P. Thompson (eds) *Narrative and Genre: Contexts and Types of communication.* p. 23 – 45. New Brunswick, NJ: Transaction Publishers

Proschan, Frank. (2007). "Field Work and social Work: Folklore as Helping Profession". In *Public Folklore,* (Eds). Baron, R & Nick Spitzer. Jackson: University Press of Mississippi. pp. 145 – 158.

Robert M. Emerson, Ed. (1983). *Contemporary Field Research.* Boston: Little Brown.

Robert, E. M., R. I. Fretz, and L. I. Shaw. (1995). *Writing ethnographic fieldnotes.* Chicago: University of Chicago Press.

Rosaldo Renato. (1989). *Culture and truth: The Ranking of Social Analysis*. Boston: Beacon.

Rossman, G. B. and Rallis, S. F. (1998). *Learning in the Field. An Introduction to Qualitative Research*. Thousand Oaks, CA: Sage.

Rouveral, A J. (2005). "Trying to be Good: Lessons in Oral History performance." In Dealla Pollock, Ed. *Remembering: Oral History Performance*. New York: Palgrave Macmillan.

Rubin and Rubin, (1995:273). Rubin, H. and Rubin, I. (1995) *Qualitative Interviewing. The Art of Hearing Data*. Thousand Oaks, CA: Sage.

Sampson, H., & Thomas, M. (2003). Risk and responsibility. *Qualitative Research, 3*(2), 165–189.

Sanjek, Roger. Ed. (1990b). *Fieldnotes: The Making of Anthropology*. Ithaca, NY.: Cornell University Press.

Sicherman, Carol. (Autumn, 1998). "Revolutionizing the Literature Curriculum at the University of East Africa: Literature and the Soul of the Nation", *Research in African Literatures*, Vol. 29, No. 3, pp. 129-148 Published by: Indiana University Press Stable URL: *http://www.jstor.org/stable/3820624*

Silverman, D. (1997). *Interpreting Qualitative Data: methods for analysing talk, text & interaction*. London: Sage Publications.

Smith, A. Deavere. (1993). *Fires in the Mirror*. Crown Heights, Brooklyn and Other Identities. New York: Anchor.

Soyinka Wole. (1978). *Myth, Literature and the African world*. London: Cambridge University.

Stemler, Steve. (2001). An overview of content analysis. *Practical Assessment, Research & Evaluation*, 7(17). Retrieved May 21, 2012 from *http://PAREonline.net/getvn.asp?v=7&n=17*

Strauss, A., and J. Corbin. (1990). *Basics of qualitative research: Grounded theory procedures*. Newbury Park, CA: Sage.

Straus, A. & Corbin, J. (1997). *Basics of qualitative research: grounded theory procedures and techniques*. Newbury Park: Sage Publications..

Temple, B. (1997). Watch your tongue: issues in translation and cross-cultural research. *Sociology*, 31(3), 607-618.

Thomson, P. (1978). *The Voice of the Past*. Oral History, Oxford: Oxford University Press. (2nd ed. 1988).

Todorov, Tzvetan. (1969). *Grammaire du Décaméron*. The Hague: Mouton.

Treweek, G., & Linkogle, S. (Eds.). (2000). *Danger in the field: Risk and ethics in social research*, pp. 8–25. London: Routledge.

Trochim, William M.K. (2006). *Research Methods Knowledge Base*. *http://www.socialresearchmethods.net/kb/positvsm.php*,

Truzzi, Marcello. (1974). *Verstehen: Subjective Understanding in the Social Sciences*. Reading, Mass.: Addison-Wesley.

Turner, in V. Yow. (1997). "Do I Like Them Too Much?" Effects of Oral History Interview on the Interviewer and Vice versa", *The Oral History Review*, 24.1; 55-79

Vansina, Jan. (1985). *Oral Tradition as History*. Nairobi: Heinemann Kenya.

Wales Katie. (2001) in *A Dictionary of Stylistics*, 2nd ed. Pearson.

Wanjiku, Kabira, and Karega Mutahi. (1988). *Gikuyu Oral Literature.* Nairobi: Heinemann.

Wanjiku, Kabira.M. (1983). *The Oral Artist.* Nairobi, Heinemann Educational publishers.

Wasamba P. (2004). "Nyatiti and Enaga Praise Poetry: Perspectives and Insights." *The Nairobi Journal of Literature. No.2.* pp 1 – 9.

_____. (2005). "Preservation of Oral Literature through Research". *The Nairobi Journal of Literature. No. 3.* pp 1 – 7.

_____. (2007). "Marching Backwards into the Future: Oral Literature in the Cyberspace" in *Chemichemi: International Journal of School of Humanities and Social Sciences,* Volume 4 Number 1 Kenyatta University.

_____. (2007). "Magic or Mirage: The efficacy of Nvivo7 in Oral Literature Research." *African Affairs Journal,* Hankuk University, pp185 – 212.

_____. (2009). "Fieldwork in a conflicted society: A contemporary researcher's ethical dilemma". *International Journal of African Renaissance Studies - Multi-, Inter- and Transdisciplinarity* Volume 4, Issue 2, pp. 193-204.

_____. (2009). The concept of heroism in Samburu moran ethos. *Journal of African Cultural Studies,* Volume 21, Issue 2, pp. 145-158.

Weaver, Anna & Atkinson, Paul. (1994). *Microcomputing and Qualitative Data Analysis.* Aldershot; Brookfield, Vermont: Avebury.

White, J. (1990). Education and the Good Life: Beyond the National Curriculum. London: London Educational Studies, Kogan Page with the Institute of Education, University of London.

White, Hayden. (1980). "The Value of Narrativity in the Representation of Reality", Critical Inquiry, 7.1: 5-27

Whitehead N: (1964). 'The self-confidence of learned people is the comic tragedy of civilization" in Goldstein, K. S. *A Guide to Field Workers in Folklore*, Hatboro: Folklore Associates Inc. and London: Herbert Jenkins: xi.

Wilgus, David. K. (1973). "The Text is the Thing." *Journal of American Folklore*. 84. 242-252.

Williams Bronwyn T. and Mary L. Brydon-Miller. (2004). "Changing Directions: Participatory Action Research, Agency and Representation." *Ethnography Unbound: From theory Shock to Critical Praxis*. Ed. Stephen G. Brown and Sidney I. Dobrin. Albany: State University of New York Press.

Vansina, Jan. (1985). *Oral Tradition as History*. Nairobi: East African Educational Publishers.

Vulliamy, G. (1990). Research Outcomes: PostScript. In G. Vulliamy, K. Lewin and D. Stephens, *Doing Educational Research in Developing Countries*. London: The Falmer Press.

Index

E

F

G

H

I

J

K

L